The
CANALS
of
ENGLAND

1, a Narrow Boat locks down at Tyrley, near Market Drayton on the Shropshire Union.

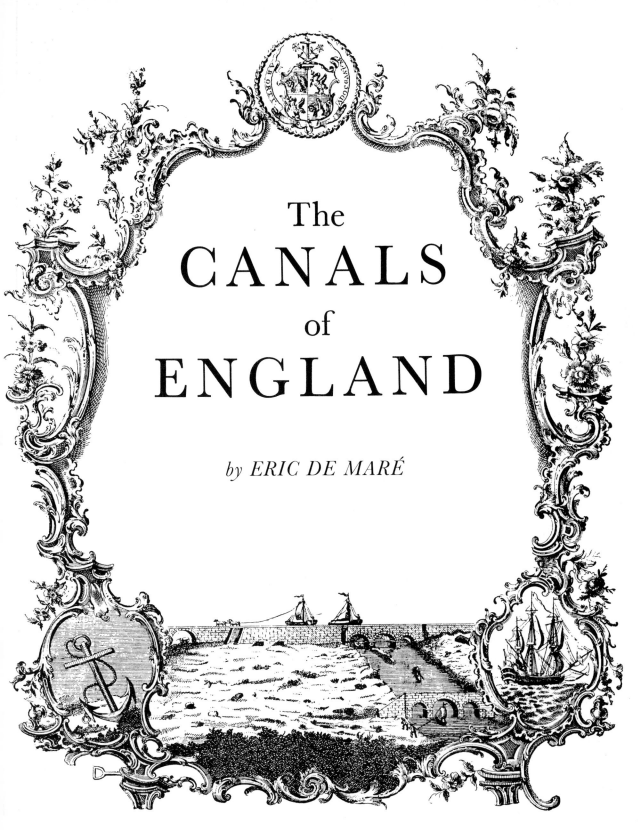

The
CANALS
of
ENGLAND

by ERIC DE MARÉ

ALAN SUTTON : 1987

ALAN SUTTON PUBLISHING
BRUNSWICK ROAD · GLOUCESTER

Copyright © Eric de Maré 1950

First published 1950
by The Architectural Press

This paperback edition published 1987

British Library Cataloguing in Publication Data

De Maré, Eric
The canals of England.
1. Canals — England — History
I. Title
386′.46′0942   HE436

ISBN 0–86299–418–7

Cover photograph by Eric de Maré

Printed in Great Britain by
The Guernsey Press Company Limited
Guernsey, Channel Islands

ACKNOWLEDGEMENTS:

The author and publishers acknowledge with thanks the help and advice given in the preparation of this book by the Inland Waterways Association and especially by its past Chairman, the late Mr. Robert F. Aickman, who read and commented on the text and checked the accuracy of the map on page 121: also by the then Secretary of the Association, the late Mr. L.T.C. Rolt, for permission to draw on much of the information he collected over many years. For photographs not taken by the author, thanks are due to Mrs. L.T.C. Rolt for No. 6 (p. 17), No. 13 (p. 19), No. 78 (p. 52), No. 172 (p. 116), to Mr. R.J.M. Sutherland for No. 33 (p. 32), No. 68 (p. 48), to the Central Office of Information for No. 41 (p. 35), No. 113 (p. 73), to the Yorkshire Post for No. 11 (p. 18), also to Messrs. Walker's Galleries, Bond Street, for the right to reproduce the drawing No. 97 (p. 64) and to Mr. C.E.R. Hadfield for advice on the bibliography (p. 120).

Contents

Illustrations

Foreword

This is virtually a facsimile reprint of a book which was first published by the Architectural Press in 1950, having already appeared in larger format as a special number of the glossy monthly *The Architectural Review*, in July 1949. The book was a pioneering effort bringing to public notice our wonderful if neglected and unap-preciated heritage of navigable waterways which had come into public ownership through the National Transport Act of 1948.

It was in the summer of that year that my wife and I explored many of the old canals (in a floating caravan based on an Army pontoon and powered by paddle wheels) on a round tour from Hampton Court up to Llangollen in North Wales and back through the Midlands. Most of the photographs reproduced here, and now in the possession of the Boat Museum at Ellesmere Port, were taken on that revelatory and fascinating journey. This reprint can therefore be seen in some degree as a work of industrial archaeology.

The changes and developments on the waterways that have occurred during the forty years which have passed since we made our journey have been considerable. They have been due largely to the efforts of that splendid body of campaigners, the Inland Waterways Association, which since its birth in 1946 has been battling for the restoration, retention, and development of British waterways and for their fullest possible use for both commerce and recreation. During four decades it has been struggling against the dead hand of bureaucracy which, by its very nature, must be uncreative and always be starved of funds by the bank-controlled Treasury.

So I am proud to have been among the handful who joined the movement at its start – a handful which has grown vigorously through the years to a present membership of more than 20,000, and which can now claim to have developed a lively Waterways Cult in this country. I am proud also to have been a friend of its two co-founders, the late Robert Aickman and Tom Rolt. Indeed, it was Tom's book, *Narrow Boat*, that inspired me to explore some of the old canals, as an early venture of my freelancing life, in a hopeful search for architectural charms surviving from the Canal Era in the form of functional bridges, aqueducts, warehouses, tunnels, locks and lock cottages, as well as Poor Man's Sculpture in such artifacts as cranes, lock paddles and bollards infinite in their variety of bold and richly textured shapes. In the event, as an architectural photographer, I was not disappointed – in spite of the unkempt state of the waterways at that time resulting from the strains of war in which many an old canal had played its useful part.

A famous early member of the IWA who became its President was the late A.P. (*Water Gypsies*) Herbert (later Sir Alan), who was obliging enough to write a lively foreword to my book, replaced for this edition by this piece. However, I would like to retain a few wise words by Herbert, for they are as relevant today as when they were written:

'It is not wholly reasonable or just to blame the Executive for the continuing lack of a national waterways policy. The Executive are servants of the public. The public should use the waterways whenever possible, whether for profit or pleasure; should demand that they are kept up as a matter of course, like roads . . . On British canals beauty and utility go hand in hand as they do not go in many places. Let the people insist on having both . . . Up, the pioneers!'

Much pioneering has been accomplished by members of the IWA – not only in words but in the volunteering deeds of digging out the silt, rebuilding locks and refurbishing derelict canals in many parts of the country. Among the successes achieved by the IWA are the retention and improvement, for example, of the Kennet and Avon (including its Crofton steam pump to working order), the Llangollen Canal, the south section of the Stratford, the Leeds and Liverpool, the Caldon, the Cheshire Ring (Lower Peak Forest, Aston and Bridgewater Canals), and the restoration of that masterpiece of early engineering, the Harecastle Tunnel on the Trent and Mersey. In March 1978 the IWA's case was greatly strengthened by the publication of the report, from the House of Commons Select Committee on Nationalised Industries, on the activities of the British Waterways Board; the Committee there approved the helpful Fraenkel Report of 1977.

What would have happened to our canal heritage if the the IWA had not come into being? Clearly, without its vigilance and energy no inter-connected system of navigable waterways would now exist. Even a part of the beautiful Thames and Severn Canal, long since abandoned and now quite derelict, has been reclaimed by a group of mudlarking enthusiasts who are hoping that one day the two great rivers will once more be joined by a navigable waterway that will penetrate the delectable Golden Valley in the Cotswolds.

Today, the problems of the old navigations must be squarely faced, for many of the narrow ones have lost the commercial value for which they were originally dug. Too many now run to and through the wrong places to be commercially viable. Unlike the wide ship canals of the Continent, many are too narrow for modern transport. The handling of most cargoes is too costly and time-consuming. On the other hand, in the handling of bulk cargoes such as coal where the continuous replenishment of stock is needed, some of the old canals can still be of economic use. Why not widen the canals? The question is often asked. The answer, strange as it may seem in these watery islands, is the difficulty of obtaining sufficient water at summit level.

Obviously, the future of most of the old narrow canals lies not in their destructive closure, which, in any case, costs more than keeping them open, but in the satisfying of amenities: as attractive features in the landscape, for tourism and holidays afloat, for angling, for tow-path walks, for wild-life conservation, for land drainage, for the supply, storage and distribution of water, and for the watering of cattle.

Now that the chips are down, we shall have to accept a future of ever-increasing leisure. What, then, will the millions who will no longer be needed in production do with their lives? Thanks to modern technology, we have reached a financial, moral and philosophical crisis. One constructive occupation for millions in the future could be the improvement of our environment, so much of which has been debased by primitive industry. Water will serve as a major element in such a revitalisation, not least for leisure activities and pleasures. Together with tree planting, conservation of top soil, and revival of small mixed farms, reconstructing the waterways could provide a valuable leisure activity. One aim could be the formation of a grand National Linear Park composed of 2,000 miles of interconnected waterways together with their towpaths and the land along their banks.

When we have come to our senses in realizing that money is not in itself a form of wealth but merely a convenient ticket system, we could enter a new and more creative culture than the sick and debt-ridden one we still endure. What is physically possible and desirable *must* be financially possible; there is no mysticism in such an obvious and simple truth. Among the possible objectives in the world of water could be that magnificent concept which is briefly described here on pages 106 to 108 – Pownall's Grand Contour Canal. With the start of that vast undertaking, the Channel Tunnel, the Grand Contour Canal need no longer be regarded as being too costly and too enormous a project to be acceptable. With the remarkable tools now available, the scheme is certainly a physical possibility; it could be one of general benefit and could inspire the whole nation with a constructive and symbolic purpose. Of course, objections are always raised against such great schemes all of which, I believe, could here be overcome.

Whatever the future may hold in waterway developments, the IWA has summarised the present position in a report, 'Waterways Survival?' published in 1980. It comments thus:

'There are more than 3100 miles of navigable inland waterways, penetrating almost every county in England, with others in Scotland and Wales. Some largely natural, others man-made, these rivers and canals are the remnants of a once even more extensive system. Its small beginnings in Roman times were added to in the Middle Ages. It burst into spectacular growth in the canal building boom or 'mania' of the late eighteenth and early nineteenth centuries. Today very few sizable places in England are without a navigable waterway, and few areas are lacking in waterway links to the rest of the country. In addition, there are many – too many – miles of derelict canals and formerly navigable rivers and drains.'

Let me end with a further quotation from A.P.H.'s original foreword.

'It was without doubt a wonderful thing to make boats climb over hills and burrow through mountains, to link the cities and the seas, the mines and the factories, by safe and silent waterways. Our ancestors in England began this business thoroughly nearly 200 years ago: and, on paper, you can go by water from almost any corner of England to almost any other. The question, now, is: Was their work wasted? Or, if it fitted their primitive times, is it now no more worth our serious attention than a camel-track or penny-farthing bicycle? Our author, at least, is not in doubt.'

Cirencester, 1987   Eric de Maré

2, Longford Bridge on the Bridgewater Canal, from an old drawing.

Introduction

The National Transport Bill became an Act on January 1, 1948. By that Act all the canals in Great Britain owned by railway companies, as well as those which had been under government control during the war, became national property. During the year some 2,000 miles of canal were taken over—almost the whole of the country's canal system.

Soon after the Act was passed representatives of the Inland Waterways Association, a private body formed in 1947 with the aim of reviving our neglected waterways, paid a visit to a high official of the Ministry of Transport. They asked him if the Ministry, having taken over the railways, had any plans for the future use of the many railway-owned canals. The high official looked astonished. So also did his callers when he cried out in a loud voice, "Oh, do we get them too?"

The anecdote illustrates the extraordinary ignorance among the public about one of our most valuable, and yet most abused, national assets—the Cinderella of the transport services. It is generally believed that inland transport by water is obsolete and that the canals now concern only a dying race of boatmen and a few melancholy antiquarians. This attitude is understandable, because, thanks to a hundred years of poor organization, neglect and, indeed, deliberate sabotage by vested interests, our waterways are not merely in bad condition, but are technically out-of-date by many decades. In fact, some of them have changed very little since the days of the Industrial Revolution.

Nevertheless, inland water transport as such is by no means obsolete. This is proved by Continental countries where modern inland waterways flourish under state control. That our own waterways, in spite of their condition, continue to carry a surprising amount of traffic shows the tenacious vitality of this kind of transport. The vitality is due to the cheapness of water transport for certain types of goods, which has been variously estimated at between 14 and 30 per cent. less than rail. The cheapness is due to the low friction of movement in water. A single horse can move 2 tons on level road, 10 tons by rail and 80 tons by water.

It must be understood, too, that inland waterways, whether navigable river or artificial cut, have other uses than that of carrying commercial traffic. They should now be considered, as they never yet have been, as part of the whole nation-wide system of water supply, conservation and drainage. In addition, they form a landscape amenity, are the habitat of fish and other wild life, and in agricultural districts are valuable for irrigation and the watering of cattle. They could become splendid grounds for pleasure boating and provide in their leafy towpaths a paradise for country walkers. This use of waterways for pleasure is no minor matter in view of the coming of the holidays-with-pay scheme and the expectation of increasing leisure as mechanization of industry grows.

Two wars have shown that, as an alternative to rail and road during times of stress, the canals are of the greatest use. From the point of view of military defence alone, canal revival might therefore be justified. In these days of road and rail congestion more benefit would be derived by expenditure on the waterways at the present time than on any other form of transport. There is every reason why we should revive them. Now that most are nationalized, revival should be far easier to achieve than it was in the past, for they can be regarded as a whole and integrated with other means of transport as part of a long-term national transport plan. The whole subject of inland navigation thus comes up for reassessment.

This book explains how canals are made and how they work, and it discusses the past, present and future of our waterways. The text is supported by old prints from the author's collection and by a set of photographs, most of which he took during a 600 mile tour through a dozen canals in 1948 from London to Llangollen and back. The pictures reveal how many architectural and scenic delights our canals possess. Many of these may not long survive—a possibility which makes their present recording the more worth while.

The camera has tried especially to capture the superb sculptural forms, textural patterns, and the occasional drama of the canal vernacular, whether this is expressed in an intimate lengthman's cottage, a grand Telford aqueduct, the gearing of a lock paddle, or the entrance to a tunnel with its sinister intimations of a John Martin hell within.

It is often thought that canals pass in endless straight lines between nightmare perspectives of industrial squalor. They sometimes do so, but by far their greater length winds sweetly through the remotest unspoiled countryside—some like the Shropshire Union and the Lancaster, across the finest landscapes of England. These Stately Roads, as Wordsworth called them, are still as wonderful today as when he wrote of them:

> The footpath faintly marked, the horse-track wild
> Have vanished—swallowed up by stately roads
> Easy and bold, that penetrate the gloom
> Of Britain's farthest glens. The Earth has lent
> Her waters, Air her breezes; and the sail
> Of traffic glides with ceaseless intercourse,
> Glistening along the low and woody dale;
> Or, in its progress, on the lofty side
> Of some bare hill, with wonder kenned from far.

Because canals generally run far from main roads, they are rarely visited, and their structures and scenes are almost unknown except to those whose lives are connected with water transport. We are now beginning to discover a lost world. It is there for us to use, if we will, for our economic advantage and our pleasure.

3, City Basin, Regent's Canal from an engraving of 1828.

12

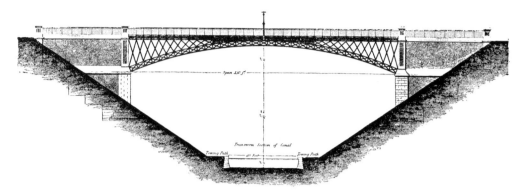

4, cast iron bridge over the Birmingham Canal at Galton designed by Telford.

Chapter 1: How Canals Work

That most vivid personality in the story of canals, James Brindley, likened uncontrolled water to a furious giant, but, said he, " if you lay the giant flat upon his back he loses all his force, and becomes completely passive, whatever his size may be." This chapter describes how to lay the giant on his back.

Canals and Rivers

Waterways can be divided into three kinds: (1) Rivers which are naturally navigable; (2) Rivers which have been made navigable by artificial means such as locks, embanking and dredging, called Canalized Rivers; (3) Artificial Cuts or Canals. Most people know something about our large rivers which, after the decay of the Roman roads, formed for centuries the chief communications through wild and impassable country. It is not to them, except incidentally, that this treatise is devoted, but to that great but little-known canal system covering the whole of England* and linking most of our rivers—the system which started in 1760 with Brindley's Bridgewater Canal and virtually concluded in 1838 with the completion of the London to Birmingham Railway. Within about eighty years roughly 3,000 miles of canal were dug, authorized by some 300 Acts of Parliament. This was the great Canal Era which made the Industrial Revolution possible.

From the start the great rivers with their seaports formed the bases on which the whole inland navigation system was built. When Brindley's fame was at its height, however, it was generally thought, owing to the poor methods of river conservancy of the time, that natural waterways were obsolete from the point of view of transport. Brindley, always a fanatic, maintained that the only use of any river was, as he pointed out to a House of Commons Committee, " to supply canals with water." Since Brindley's day, rivers have recovered some of their original importance and

* The Scottish and English canal systems are quite independent and are not linked at any point. The Scottish system comprising about fourteen navigations, four of them major ones, is by no means unimportant, but owing to the vastness of the whole subject, the palette is here restricted to the English system alone.

any broad schemes for improving inland navigation in the future must consider canals and rivers as interdependent.

Canals have the advantage over rivers of providing still water and are less liable to interrupt traffic by flood and drought. Though canals are often tortuous, rivers are even more so. Nor do canals need pilotage as do many rivers, and they provide the only form of transport which is substantially unaffected by snow or fog. On the other hand, canals are more liable to freeze in winter than are rivers owing to their still water, and lockage is often heavy, thus slowing down speed considerably.

Canals have been defined as supplying the deficiencies of natural waterways by their construction " in places where rivers are not available, or to provide a passage where serious obstacles to navigation exist in a river, or to connect two river navigations by surmounting the water-parting of their basins." They can be divided into two types: (1) Arterial, those which connect two river basins or valleys, and (2) Lateral, those which run parallel to rivers and follow the same valley in their course. The latter are easy to execute, the former less so, because they must be led through or over high ridges and need many locks, deep cuttings and possibly tunnels, and they are not easily supplied with water. A canal may, of course, be lateral at some part of its length and arterial at another.

In this country no standard dimensions for canals have ever been fixed. The canals grew in a haphazard way, built originally to serve regional needs and to accommodate traditional types of craft from local rivers, but in general there are two systems of canals—the narrow with locks 7 ft. wide and the broad with locks 14 to 18 ft. wide. The most common dimensions of narrow canals are, at least in theory, 40 to 45 ft. surface width, 25 ft. bottom width, 5 ft. depth.

Speed of travel on the canals is limited, not so much by the force of the motive power of the boats, whether motor or horse, as by the section of the cut. Too narrow a sectional area will cause considerable resistance, and from the point of view of water resistance alone, the wider the section the better. Silting caused by bank erosion, considerably aggravated these days by motor boats, tends to increase resistance. The remedy for this lies in strengthening the banks and in proper dredging. At present dredging is universally inadequate even on such busy thoroughfares as the Grand Union, and on many lines pathetic attempts are made to relieve the worst spots with manually operated " spoons," a sad symptom of waterway impoverishment.

Types of Canal Vessels

By far the most common type of boat used on the canals is the Narrow Boat or Monkey Boat, 70 ft. long by 7 ft. wide, built either of wood or steel. The Narrow Boat is usually worked in pairs by a family which lives in the stern cabins. The leading boat, mostly driven by a diesel nowadays, though sometimes horse-drawn, tows the rear or butty boat. In the days when the canals were better maintained than they are today and before the power-driven craft had sucked so much of the soil from the banks into the bottom of the channels, these boats would carry 30 to 35 tons each. Now the average loading is 25 tons for the motor boat and 30 tons for the butty. A pair of narrow boats will travel 35 miles a day if power-driven and 25 miles if horse-drawn. On the broad canals, such as the Grand Union, these boats lock through together side by side, whereas in the narrow canals each boat goes through separately, making for slower progress. Horses are now mostly used for short hauls in the Black Country area to pull the so-called Day Boats, which contain no living accommodation. Horse-boats travel at about 2 m.p.h. loaded, and 3 empty; motor boats travel about 1 m.p.h. faster.

The Narrow Boat

The traditional Narrow Boat is a very beautiful craft, perfectly adapted to its purpose. It is more or less standardized, though there are minor regional differences. Most people are now familiar with the vivid decorations of canal boats—the roses and landscapes with their Carpathian castles which constitute the one remaining folk art alive in England today.

The origin of this art is obscure. Some say it came with the gypsies from the Carpathians, others that the main inspiration for the landscapes were Victorian oleographs of Windsor Castle, while a third theory holds that it goes right back to Norman times, the distinctive eastern flavour being brought by Crusaders. This folk art is a kind of painter's short-hand and is executed with surprising speed and skill; it has its firm conventions but within them the imagination of the artist has considerable scope. The art is tending to die out, and is not, unfortunately, receiving encouragement from the new controlling bureaucracy. The boaters at one time also had their own mode of dress, notably the bonnets and wide skirts of the women and the brightly coloured woven belts of the men; to-day these traditional garments are rarely seen.

Originally most craft were owned by the boatmen themselves who took great pride in the condition and appearance of their possessions. Today there are very few owner-boatmen, or Number Ones, left on the cut; the ineluctable process of centralization has brought the boatmen to the state of a dependent employee working at piece rates for large and small carrying companies, many of which have now come under national ownership.

A modification of the narrow boat is found on the Huddersfield Broad Canal and the Calder and Hebble Navigation. These are 58 ft. long by 7 ft. beam so that they may pass the short locks found on these navigations.

Another type of fairly common boat is the Wide Boat, 70 ft. by 10 ft., carrying 50 tons. This is found mainly on the lower part of the Grand Union. There are also the barge and lighter of varying dimensions, the largest of which are those often seen on the Thames. On the Aire and Calder, compartment boats, or Tom Puddings, are used. These are oblong iron boxes towed in trains up to 32 in number by steam tugs—a development of the early Shropshire tub-boats. Other types of craft to meet special conditions and needs are the Fen Lighters, the Severn Trows and the Norfolk Wherries which, apart from the Thames Sailing Barges, are the last surviving inland sailing craft. There is also a special type of wide boat still in use on the semi-derelict Basingstoke Canal.

Ship Canals

A special sort of canal is the Ship Canal which can be defined as a waterway constructed to provide deep water access to the sea for old ports, or to convert inland towns into seaports. The oldest ship canal in the Kingdom is that running

from Topsham to Exeter. It was built in 1544, but was considerably enlarged in 1820 by Telford. Another ship canal carried out by Telford is that between Gloucester and the Severn estuary at Sharpness, begun in 1818. It provides a valuable, direct and still-water navigation to Gloucester in place of the 26 miles of tortuous river with its rapid tidal currents.

The most famous and busy of ship canals is, of course, the Manchester Ship Canal which was opened by Queen Victoria in 1894. Its opening can be considered as a major event in the development of British industry and brought a temporary revival of all inland navigation. It is a grand piece of engineering and is particularly interesting because, itself the *last* major event in canal construction in this country, it can be regarded as a development of the Bridgewater Canal, virtually the *first* major event, since it inaugurated the Canal Era.

Typical examples of traditional landscapes with their stylized castles which are painted both inside and outside the cabins of Narrow Boats. 5, 6, two examples by Nurser of Braunston. 7, panel by Tooley of Banbury. 8, 10, the traditional can and dipper of the Narrow Boat with their brilliant decoration of roses; the background is dark green, the roses are yellow, pink and scarlet. 9, the underside of the dipper. The origin of this folk art is obscure.

Water Supply

Water supply is the basic problem in canal construction. For lateral canals the problem is easily solved, since these derive their supply from rivers at points well below their source. For arterial canals the problem is more difficult.

Water conservancy has been defined as " the scientific treatment and regulation of all water received in these islands from its first arrival in the form of dew or rain till its final disappearance in the ocean." At present we make pitiful use of this gift from heaven and suffer too often and quite needlessly from drought, flood and inadequate drainage. Nor do we make enough use of it for proper rural supplies or for transport. Through lack of scientific control, too much water is allowed to run to waste into the seas. Nature supplies us abundantly with water. A great ridge runs

11   12

Canal boat types. 11, a train of Tom Puddings on the Aire and Calder Navigation. 12, ice-breakers at Norbury Junction on the Shropshire Union Canal; when the ice is thick it is broken by rocking these boats from side to side, the crews standing on the slatted platforms and gripping the rails which run above the centres of the boats—a quaint anomaly in this machine age, and one which is typical of our neglected canals. 13, the remains of one of the small tunnel boats at Worsley Basin, used at one time for mining the Duke of Bridgewater's colliery. 14, a horsedrawn ice-breaker of steel on the Stratford-on-Avon Canal, used sometimes for clearing a passage through the thick duck-weed when a rare pleasure boat demands a thoroughfare. 15, an old print of 1796 from Fulton's " Treatise on the Improvement of Canal Navigation," of a Market, or Passage, Boat of the day.

like a backbone nearly the whole length of the country from north to south. Springs and rainfalls flow down on each side to the opposite coasts. As many as twenty-two canals now cross and re-cross this ridge forming connections between the rivers of east and west. There is a secondary water parting running east and west in the south of England, which separates the rivers flowing into the English Channel from those flowing into the Bristol Channel and the Thames. The rivers of England and Wales are thereby divided by these two partings into three main systems.

This natural arrangement was, of course, the factor which most influenced the canal constructors in the laying out of their routes. Another factor also influenced them to some extent, though they were only half-conscious of it. That is the contour line of 300 ft. which runs all the way from Newcastle down to Southampton, taking in Manchester, Coventry and Bristol and running as far east as Hertford. This factor is made full use of in Mr. Pownall's remarkable Grand Contour Canal scheme described later.

Most of the water on all canals has to be derived from a point near the summit level, which is usually above the 400 ft. contour. This means that springs and

13   14

15

streams supplying the canal must be above that level. In summer the springs and streams are often inadequate and, to overcome this, one or more reservoirs are built which will retain the surplus water provided by the winter rains. The summit level should, obviously, be as low as possible to make water supply easier and to avoid unnecessary locks. In most cases a cutting or tunnel is needed at the summit level, in which case, with good luck, springs are found during excavations to supply a considerable amount of water. The summit pound can itself, if long enough, act as a reservoir. If a sufficient supply of water at the summit is unobtainable and there is no other way out of the difficulty, pumping up from a lower level must be resorted to. Water can also be pumped up from deep springs or artesian wells, and possibly from mines liable to flood. The various methods can be combined. " In this way," as Mr. L. T. C. Rolt writes in his report on Inland Waterways published for the Association for Planning and Regional Reconstruction, " the canal system is very closely linked with the drainage and water supply system of large areas. It represents

B

an elaborate mechanism of water conservation in precisely those areas most susceptible to drought."

As well as initially filling a new canal, the water supply must thereafter maintain a steady contribution to replenish losses. Loss of water in a canal occurs for these reasons: passage of boats through locks, evaporation, leakage through the sides and bottom of the canal, leakage of lock-gates, turning water out of the pounds for repairs.

Canals are formed of level stretches or pounds situated between locks at various heights, locks being the most common method of overcoming differences of level. It is the passage of boats through locks which takes most of the water. An essay on canals by one, W. O'Brien, which won a prize offered by the Canal Association in 1858, explains the matter clearly:

" The loss of water caused by the passage of a boat through a lock is as follows:

W=L plus B, when the boat ascends.

W, loss of water; L, lockful or prism of water having the area of lock for its basis and the total fall of the lock for its height; B, volume of water displaced by the boat.

When the boat descends, the loss is W=L minus B.

A boat going up or down takes W water, whatever be the number of locks, each lockful taken from the summit level going all the way down. If a boat goes up to the summit level and down again on the other side, it causes an expenditure equal to 2L, supposing the boat's load not to vary materially in the course of the journey.

If the descending boat is immediately followed by one ascending, or *vice versa*, the loss is still the same, or only L per boat.

Sometimes, in steep ascents, several locks are joined together without any intermediate pound; the cost of construction is lessened thereby; but in that case an ascending boat requires as many locksful as there are locks, in addition to the volume displaced by the boat, or

nL plus B,

n being the number of adjacent locks.

In descending, the loss of water is L minus B as before."

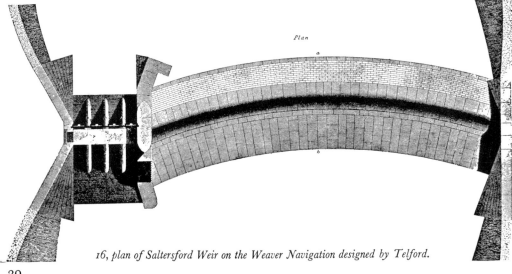

16, plan of Saltersford Weir on the Weaver Navigation designed by Telford.

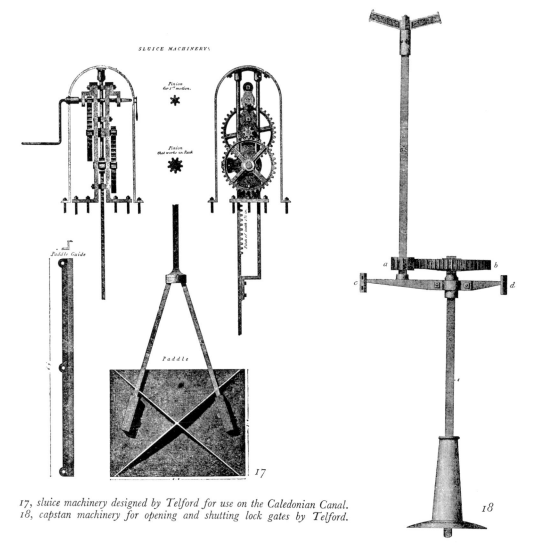

17, sluice machinery designed by Telford for use on the Caledonian Canal.
18, capstan machinery for opening and shutting lock gates by Telford.

The amount of water used in lockage thus varies with the displacement factor, and a loaded boat will consume more water than an empty one when locking up, but an empty one will consume more than a loaded one when locking down. To counter the inequalities of water level in different pounds caused by boats of different displacement, and also to deal with flood water, with the effects of leakage or with variations in depths of locks, weirs are provided at each lock.

Various methods have been evolved to save water used in lockage. These are described in the Rolt Report as follows:

(*a*) Waiting Turns. The most economical use of water is secured if a boat moving up a flight of locks is next succeeded by a boat travelling in the opposite direction. It leads to considerable delay unless traffic is heavy and regular, but is sometimes enforced in time of drought.

(*b*) Side Ponds. These consist of small reservoirs built beside each lock at a level midway between that of the upper and lower pounds and connected to the lock by means of a paddle or sluice. A descending boat entering a full lock first discharges the water from the lock into the side pond until lock and side pond levels equalize with the lock half empty. The side pond paddle is then closed, and the remainder of the water in the lock is discharged into the canal below in the ordinary way. Similarly, an ascending boat entering the empty lock first half-fills the lock from the side pond before drawing the remainder from the canal above. In each case half a lock of water is saved. Many of the locks on the Grand Union Canal employ this system.

(*c*) Paired Locks. In this case duplicate locks, side by side, employ the principle described above, one acting as a side pond to the other.

(*d*) Pumping Back. The installation of pumping units at each lock or compact flight of locks which return lockage water from the lower to the higher levels.

For preventing leakage through the bottom of a canal the great standby has always been, and remains, puddled clay.

Appliances for Overcoming Change of Level

Most of the early canals were built as much for drainage and irrigation as for navigation, and it was not until the invention of the lock that canals came into their own. No one knows who originated the lock, though the invention is generally attributed to Leonardo, who round about 1488 prepared a scheme for the Duke of Milan for supplying Milan with water by means of a new canal. The canal, called Mortesana, is 200 miles long and navigable throughout. Says an eighteenth century writer: " Leonardo surmounted all opposition and happily achieved what some may think miraculous, rendering *hills* and valleys *navigable* with security." Some say, nevertheless, that the first lock must be attributed to Visconti, who in 1439 connected two lakes for the purpose of transporting marble for Milan Cathedral.

Be that as it may, the lock revolutionized inland navigation and thereafter many lock canals were built in the Continental countries. In England, however, canal development was slow. Apart from the lock canal of Exeter the only canal to be constructed before the great boom opened with the Bridgewater Canal, was the St. Helens, or Sankey, Canal from the Mersey to St. Helens, completed through the efforts of the " commercial and enterprising inhabitants of Liverpool " in 1760.

Locks.—The most common appliance for overcoming a change of level is the lock. A lock consists of a chamber at each end of which there is a gate or pair of

19, double lock and east entrance to Islington Tunnel on the Regent's Canal. From an engraving of 1827 made from a drawing by Thomas Shepherd.

gates. When the chamber is " empty," that is with its water level with the lower pound, a boat going up can enter it. The lower gates are shut and the sluices closed. The sluices on the upper gates are then opened, and the chamber fills, so raising the boat to the level of the upper pound. The upper gates can then be opened and the boat proceeds on its way. On descent the process is reversed.

The early types of lock were often constructed entirely of timber and there is another old type, not yet totally extinct, which has sloping turf sides with a row of piles driven into the foot of the slope to confine vessels to their proper positions when locking down.

On the Shropshire Union Canal at Beeston near Chester, there are two locks designed by Telford with sides of cast-iron plates bolted together and resting on piles, the reason being that they are built in quicksand. The most common material for the sides of lock chambers, however, is either brick or masonry.

Lock-gates are usually of timber having the back of the heel-post of semi-circular section to rotate in a hollow quoin. Sometimes cast-iron gates are found.

The plan shape of locks is usually rectangular. On the Oxford Canal and on the Lower Avon Navigation you can find a few examples of the diamond-shaped lock having double the width of the usual narrow boat lock. The object of this is to equate the amount of water the diamond lock passes with that passed by the ordinary deeper locks above it, for diamond locks are only built where the rise is small. Even circular and crescent locks have been built.

As a rule locks are not built to give a fall of more than 6 to 8 ft., as they would otherwise consume an excessive amount of water and the lower gates would become too large to move by hand. The largest canal lock in England is the entrance lock to the Manchester Ship Canal at Eastham, measuring 600 ft. by 70 ft. and worked, of course, by machine. The smallest locks, at least in width, are those on the old disused Shropshire Canal between Wappenshall Junction and Trench, measuring over 80 ft. long but only 6 ft. 4 in. wide. They were built to take four tub-boats at a time, each measuring 20 ft. by 6 ft. 2 in. These old tub-boats were drawn by a horse in trains of twenty at a time. The stretch of canal with the largest number of locks per miles lies between Worcester and Tardebigge on the Worcester and Birmingham Canal. Here there are fifty-eight locks in 16 miles, which include the famous flight of thirty at Tardebigge.

Staircase locks, or Risers, are locks arranged in a flight without intermediate pounds, where the lower gates of one lock act as the upper gates of the next. Risers are used where the slope of ground is steep and consume much water when boats are ascending. Another disadvantage is that boats cannot pass each other during the locking through. A fine example of staircase locks is the set of five at Bingley on the Leeds and Liverpool Canal, which give a total lift of 59 ft.

Throughout most of the English canal system, lock-gates and sluice paddles are worked by hand by the boat crews. Paddles are usually moved by rack and pinion by means of a portable windlass. Sometimes they are on the gate itself, sometimes at the side, when they are termed Ground Paddles, but usually, at least on the upper end of locks, paddles are found both on the gates and at the sides. In the old days a ratchet and crowbar system was used, only a few examples of which now survive.

Where two canals join you will find a so-called stop-lock. This generally has two chambers in order to deal with any differences in water level between the two canals.

One canal may be higher than the other one day but lower the next; hence, the need for two chambers to deal with either situation. The variation of levels between two canals at stop-locks is generally no more than a few inches.

A very rare type of stop-lock can be seen at King's Norton where the Stratford Canal joins the Worcester and Birmingham. This is called a Guillotine or Portcullis lock and is a fine piece of early cast-iron engineering. In this type only one chamber is needed, the gates being vertical plates raised and lowered on a frame by a windlass, The only other examples are at two locks on the disused Shropshire Tub-boat Canal, though modernized versions have now been installed on the Nene and the Ouse.

Vertical Lifts.—Another method of overcoming differences of level is the vertical lift. Though many ingenious proposals have been put forward from time to time, only one is now in actual use. This is the famous Anderton Lift between the River Weaver and the Trent and Mersey Canal. The arguments in favour of lifts are that they save water and speed up traffic. Arguments against them are that both capital and running costs are high. Steam, hydraulic or electric power is needed to run them as well as attendants. In general, except where change of level is naturally very steep, lifts as opposed to locks are not justified.

A vertical lift was erected at Tardebigge on the Worcester and Birmingham in 1809 and there were seven others built in 1836 on the Grand Western Canal between Taunton and Loudwell. Nothing remains of any of these lifts today.

The Anderton, opened in 1875, is, however, still very active. " This lift," explains an engineer of the last century, " raises and lowers the canal boats through a height of 50 ft., between the River Weaver and the Trent and Mersey Canal, being connected with the latter by a wrought-iron aqueduct. The boats are enclosed in a water-tight trough, and remain afloat during the whole operation. . . . The caissons or troughs are capable of holding two of the narrow boats in use on the canal, and the operation of entering, lowering, and opening the gates and passing out can be performed in from ten to twelve minutes. The waste of water is 6 in. deep over the area of the trough, eleven-twelfths of the stroke being performed by means of the weight of this water, and the remaining power being supplied by a small engine working an accumulator. As the lift has two troughs which are in equilibrium until the 6 in. extra of water is put in, one always ascending and the other descending, it is ready for either up or down traffic, and when vessels from both sides arrive at once it acts as a double lock."

Inclined Plane Lifts.—The inclined plane lift has also been the subject of much ingenious thought, but, like the vertical lift, has never been used to any great extent. It has been defined as " a ship-railway, by which a large tank full of water, supported on wheels, is drawn up an inclined railroad, or the boat is drawn out of the water and carried on a cradle."

Remains of an inclined plane lift built in 1900, which was worked by steam, may still be seen at Foxton on the Grand Union Canal. The appliance consisted of two caissons, each mounted on ten wheels, and running on five rails parallel to each other. The caissons were pulled up laterally by wire ropes, the one balancing the other and the extra power coming from a stationary winding engine. The length of the plane was 307 ft. and the rise 75 ft. 2 in. It proved too expensive to run as a head of steam had to be maintained whether the lift was in use or not.

(*Opposite*) 20, *illustrations from Fulton's " Treatise on the Improvement of Canal Navigation " of 1796, which show his proposals for lifts to take trains of small boats. Top, the double inclined plane lift; at the top is a pit in which a tub moves up and down " into which water is drawn from the upper canal in order to create a power to put the machine in motion." Centre, the well house. Below, a medium plane for a small ascent, being a medium between locks and planes, where a water-wheel provides the motive power. On page 26 are details of the double inclined plane lift*

24

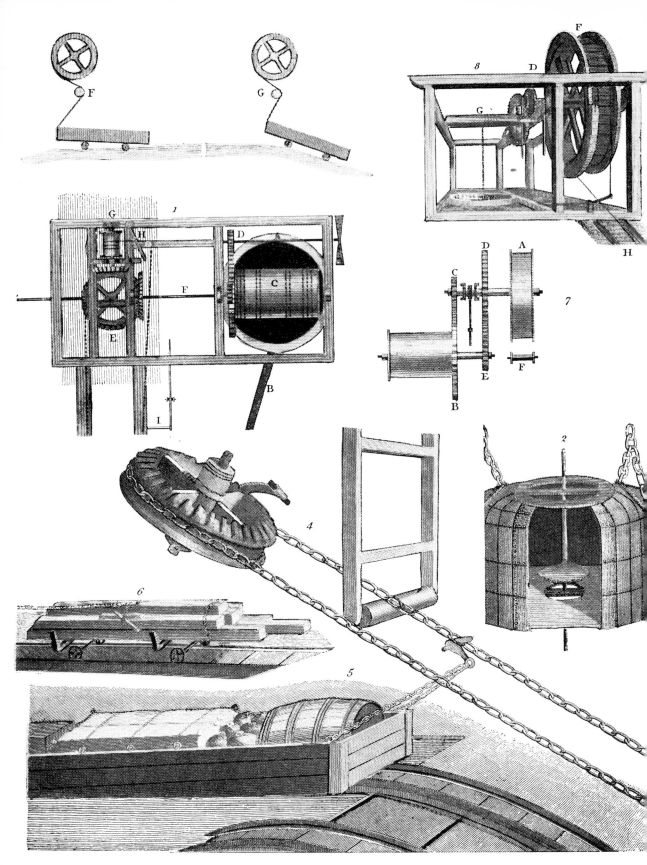

21, details of Fulton's double inclined plane lift.

22

22, the Anderton Hydraulic Lift built in 1875, which raises boats 50 feet up from the River Weaver on to the Trent and Mersey Canal. 23, a vertical lift as proposed by Robert Fulton in his treatise of 1796, in which he pleads for the use of smaller type canals taking small boats of two to five tons capacity worked in trains; he designed machinery for these small canals which would eliminate all locks and aqueducts.

23

There was another inclined plane lift at one time at Trench on the old Shropshire Tub-boat Canal passing tub-boats measuring 20 ft. by 6 ft. 2 in. This was built towards the end of the eighteenth century and consisted of two lines of rails, on each of which ran a trolley raised and lowered by a wire rope and carrying one tub-boat at a time. Here again the descending trolley balanced the weight of the ascending one, the extra power being supplied by a stationary winding engine. The length of the plane was 227 yds. and the rise 73 ft. 6 in.

There have been others such as that built at one time at Coalport, similar to the Trench Lift, with a vertical rise of 213 ft., while on the old Bude Canal all changes of level were accomplished by inclined planes to take 4-ton tub-boats.

If and when the canals are modernized, it is possible that electric power may bring back the vertical and inclined plane lift in certain cases, for today power can be switched on or off as required. There is no need now to maintain a permanent head of steam.

The Track

Our essay winner of 1858 writes:

" In laying out a line, the following conditions should be fulfilled:

    (1) To avoid porous soils;

    (2) To avoid passing through expensive property, except for the establishment of basins in commercial centres;

27

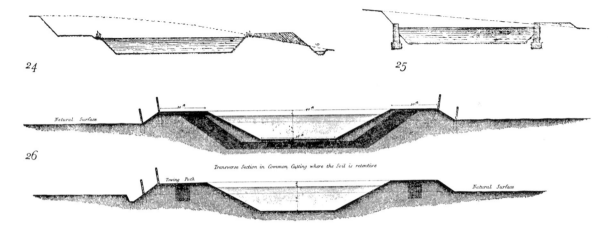

24 25

26

24, 25, sections showing the change in methods of the construction of canals reproduced from a prize essay on canals by W. O'Brien published in 1858. 24, the original style of execution and 25, the improved method. 26, two sections of the Birmingham and Liverpool Junction Canal, now the Shropshire Union, as designed by Telford.

(3) To provide a sufficient supply of water at all times by means of low levels and deep reservoirs;

(4) To dispose the line so that excavations shall compensate embankments as nearly as possible;

(5) To make the line as short as possible, sacrificing, if necessary, some of the preceding conditions, so as to obtain a saving in time and in the working expenses.

" Fig. 24 shows how canals were originally executed. Raised towing-paths are made at least on one side, frequently on both sides, with the earth dug out for the bed of the canal. The latter is set out with a slope, which is frequently 1 in 1, but which varies with the nature of the soil. At the level of the surface of the water a narrow ledge is left, on which rushes, etc., are planted to protect the banks from waves or ripples. A drain may be necessary to carry off the leakage.

" Fig. 25 shows a modification better suited for steam navigation. . . . The shores are vertical. They may be protected from the surge caused by steamers,

27, an old print of the classical façade of the south end of Sapperton Tunnel on the now derelict Thames and Severn Canal; the north end has a Gothic flavour with a castellated top (see fig. 77, page 52). The tunnel pierces the ridge which divides the two river basins and is the second longest in the country at $2\frac{1}{4}$ miles; the longest is Standedge at $3\frac{1}{10}$ miles on the Huddersfield Narrow Canal. Sapperton Tunnel was visited by George III in 1788 during its construction; it is still in a fair state of preservation though the growth of trees has altered the picture as seen here. The little canal inn at the top of the slope is still standing.

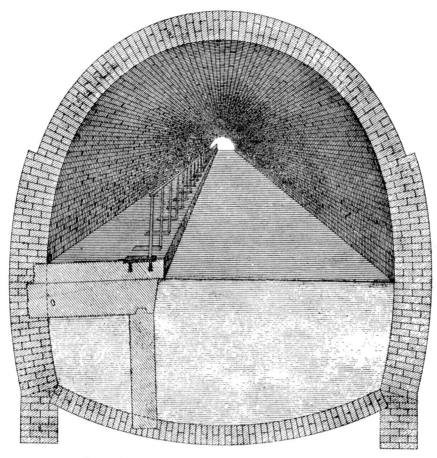

28, a sectional-cum-perspective engraving of the second Harecastle Tunnel built by Telford as an alternative to Brindley's earlier tunnel on the old Grand Trunk, now the Trent and Mersey.

either by means of a lining of beton (concrete formed with gravel and hydraulic lime) or by rough stone-work without mortar. The drift soon fills up the joints."

In principle one cannot improve on Fig. 25 for modern canals.

Tunnels, Bridges and Aqueducts

These are important incidentals in canal building and are very similar to the works needed in railway construction. Indeed the pioneering efforts of the canal engineers greatly helped the subsequent development of railways.

Tunnels.—The first main line canal tunnel built in England was Harecastle Old Tunnel on the Grand Trunk, now called the Trent and Mersey. It was begun by Brindley in 1766 but not finished until 1777, five years after Brindley's death. It is $1\frac{2}{3}$ miles long and a stupendous feat of engineering for those days. Later, with more experience and better facilities to back him, Telford constructed another tunnel alongside the old of larger dimensions and containing a towpath. The latest tunnel to be built is the Netherton, which was finished in 1858 on the Birmingham

29, *perspective, section and plan of a typical canal accommodation bridge from an engraving of 1809.*

Canal Navigations. It is about $1\frac{3}{4}$ miles long and is lit by gas—the only canal tunnel to be artificially lit. Comparison of dimensions is interesting. Old Harecastle: minimum height above water level, 5 ft. 10 in.; minimum width at water level, 18 ft. 6 in.; no towpath. Netherton: height, 15 ft. 9 in.; width, 17 ft. of waterway, 27 ft. including two towpaths.

Of the nine canal tunnels which are over a mile long, Standedge, piercing the ridge dividing the Tame and Colne valleys, on the Huddersfield Narrow Canal, is the longest of all at $3\frac{1}{10}$ miles. It is also the highest above sea level, and lies on the

[continued on page 37]

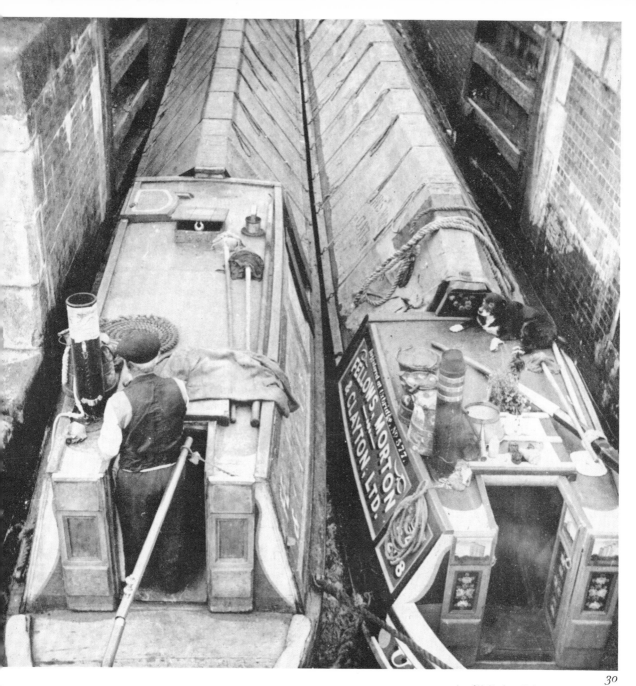

30, a pair of " *Joshers* " (or *Fellows, Morton and Clayton boats*) entering a lock among the flight of twenty-one at Hatton on the old Warwick and Birmingham Canal, now part of the Grand Union. The fit is exact for no water must be wasted. 31, the elegant form of a Narrow Boat emerges from a lock. 32, a lighter locks down at Hanwell on the Grand Union.

33, *looking up at a pier of Cotton-King Samuel Oldknow's aqueduct at Marple on Peak Forest Canal. 34, an intrepid pleasure boat crosses Telford's Chirk Aqued which carries the Welsh Section of the Shropshire Union across the River Ceriog. its passage through the tunnel into Wales the pleasure boat may find its way block by rotting branches and vegetation. No commercial craft now pass this way; for we at a time the water is undisturbed while above trains roar day and night across viaduct to Chester. 35, the park-like scene from above the entrance to Chirk Tunn 36, engraving of Chirk Aqueduct from "The Atlas to the Life of Thomas Telford The channel was originally of puddled clay but this was later changed to cast in*

33

34

32

35

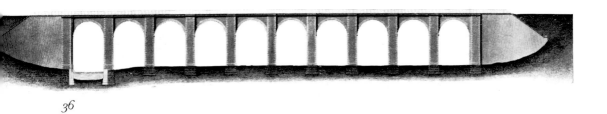

36

37

38

39

40

On facing page, views of Pontcysyllte Aqueduct, Telford's masterpiece, on the Welsh Section of the Shropshire Union. 37, a close-up of the stone piers carrying cast iron arches and trough. 38, view from the side of the turbulent Dee. 39, the trough. 40, engraving of Pontcysyllte Aqueduct from " The Atlas to the Life of Thomas Telford."

41, the Barton Swing Aqueduct built in 1893 to carry the Bridgewater Canal across the Manchester Ship Canal. 42, Brindley's Barton Aqueduct which the swing aqueduct replaced; it was built in 1761 to carry the Bridgewater Canal across the River Irwell which was later absorbed into the ship canal.

41

42

43

44

43, *a dramatic cutting near Market Drayton on Telford's Birmingham and Liverpool Junction Canal, now called the Shropshire Union or Shroppie Cut. All the elements of canal scenery are here, lock platform and balance beam, painted Narrow Boat, towpath, tree overhang and dark tunnel entrance. An artificial transport cut becomes a fine but unselfconscious piece of landscape art with its use of natural materials, rocky tree-crowned cuttings, little functional bridges and lock weirs sparkling like decorative waterfalls. 44, a picturesque towpath landscape near Braunston Junction on the Grand Union Canal.*

highest navigation in England. It was built without a towpath at the end of the eighteenth century. The second longest is the Sapperton on the now completely derelict Thames and Severn Canal, running for $2\frac{1}{8}$ miles through the ridge dividing the two river basins.

In the early tunnels towpaths were never constructed, and boats were propelled through them either by shafting or legging. Shafting consisted of pushing with a long pole against the top or sides of the tunnel and was generally used only in short tunnels. Legging was carried out by two men, one on each side of the boat lying on their backs and pushing against the tunnel sides with their feet. Later steam haulage was used, but today most boats pass through on their own power, although in Telford's Harecastle Tunnel boats are still hauled through by a strange electric tug drawing its current from an overhead cable and hauling itself along on a second cable in the bed of the channel which it picks up on a winch and then pays out astern. There are in all forty-five canal tunnels in England and Wales.

Bridges.—These are of two main sorts—Accommodation Bridges which carry roads or farm tracks across the canal, and Roving Bridges which carry the towpath itself across from one side of the canal to the other. The usual type of overline accommodation bridge is the single-arch brick or stone structure with towpath carried under it alongside the canal.

A type of bridge of special interest is that found on the Stratford-on-Avon and Staffordshire and Worcestershire Canals. It was designed to save the expense of carrying the towpath under without the need of casting off and re-attaching the tow-line. The bridge, called a Split Bridge, consists of two iron brackets cantilevered out towards each other from a brick abutment on either side. The brackets do not touch, but leave a space of about $\frac{3}{4}$ in. through which the tow-line can be slipped.

Movable bridges are fairly common and are of two kinds—those called turn, or swing bridges, which open by turning to one side on a centre and those called drawbridges which open by lifting upwards and are balanced by counter-weights. The Oxford Canal has its own special type of drawbridge and the Welsh Section of the Shropshire Union another, of a character similar to those in Van Gogh's paintings. The Gloucester and Berkeley Ship Canal also has its own type of turn bridge of extremely elegant appearance.

Canal bridges are perhaps the most beautiful and interesting of canal structures, and have the charm not merely of the variety of regional types, but also of local variety within those types. Thus, within a regional standard, as for instance Telford's little stone bridges on the Shropshire Union, you will find homogeneous style, but never mechanical repetition. Purely functional, quite unselfconscious, perfectly proportioned and fitting snugly into the landscape, these bridges have a fine monumental quality which few engineering structures have since achieved, except perhaps the modern reinforced concrete bridges of Robert Maillart. They are perfect examples of the functional tradition.

Aqueducts.—These are necessary to carry the canal track across roads, railways, rivers and streams. The earliest canal aqueduct built in England was that at Barton opened in 1761 amidst much sceptical scoffing. Designed by Brindley, it carried the Duke of Bridgewater's Canal, described by a contemporary as " an aqueduct bridge over the navigable River Irwell at the height of 38 ft. above its surface, which presented to the wondering spectators the new and surprising sight of

c*

vessels sailing aloft in the air, high above other vessels sailing below in the river."
Built of stone, the Barton Aqueduct was about 600 ft. long and 36 ft. wide, with
a waterway 18 ft. wide and 4½ ft. deep carried in a channel of puddled clay. It
remained in use and in a good state until it was superseded in 1893 by the present
Barton Swing Aqueduct needed to carry the Bridgewater Canal across the new
Manchester Ship Canal into which the River Irwell had been absorbed, while at
the same time permitting the passage of large ships.

The Barton Swing Aqueduct is an amazing feat of nineteenth century engineering.
The main girders of the swinging part are 234 ft. long and the trough it carries is
18 ft. wide and 6 ft. deep. The swinging part revolves on a central pier and, in order
to avoid the delay which would be caused by emptying and filling the trough each
time the aqueduct is opened, it is swung full of water. This is achieved by a system
of gates closing the ends both of the trough and the canal itself at the two shores.
Keeping the gates watertight was the chief problem which the engineers had to face,
and this was finally accomplished by the use of rubber-faced, tapering wedges,
weighing 12 tons each and worked by hydraulic rams. The moving structure with
its water content weighs about 1,500 tons.

Two other famous aqueducts are those at Chirk and Pontcysyllte on the Welsh
part of the Shropshire Union—the old Ellesmere Canal. Both are the work of
Telford and show a development of Brindley's technique in that the troughs they
carry are both of cast iron. Chirk was originally built with a puddled clay bed,
but this was later changed.

Chirk Aqueduct, carrying the canal over the River Ceriog, was built in 1801 of ten
stone arches. Pontcysyllte, built two years later across the River Dee, has stone piers
supporting cast-iron arches—a magnificent structure and certainly one which must

*45, Brindley's aqueduct over the River Sow at Milford on the
Staffordshire and Worcestershire Canal. 46, Barton Swing
Aqueduct being swung full of water; the whole weighs 1,500 tons.*

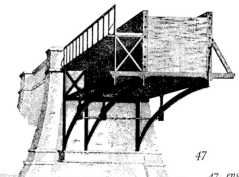

47, engraving of 1796 of a cast iron aqueduct. 48, an old print of Rolle Aqueduct on the Torridge Canal, Devonshire, now defunct.

be included among the Seven Wonders. (It is perhaps time to list these Seven Wonders of the Canals. They are: Pontcysyllte Aqueduct, the Barton Swing Aqueduct, the Anderton Lift, the Bingley Five-Rise Lock, Standedge Tunnel—all of which have been mentioned. To these add: the great Burnley Embankment on the Leeds and Liverpool Canal and the remarkable flight of twenty-nine locks with their long side ponds at Devizes on the Kennet and Avon.)

Inns and Cottages

Buildings which are part and parcel of canal economy and can therefore legitimately come under this section are the canal inns and the cottages of the toll clerks, lock-keepers and lengthmen. (Lengthmen are canal employees in charge of a particular length of waterway.)

The photographs will tell more about the architectural interest of these buildings than words, but a good colourful impression which describes the purpose and atmosphere of canal inns can be found in L. T. C. Rolt's *Narrow Boat*:

" It was evening by the time we reached the bottom to moor by the village of Napton-on-the-Hill. . . . It was here that we found our first canal inn. Approached by a rough track, it stood in the fields on the side of the canal away from the village, and, with outbuildings grouped around the house, it looked like a small farm, except for the faded sign of *The Bull and Butcher* over the door. Inns such as this fulfil the same purpose as the great posting-houses of coaching days, for they are recognized ' stages ' on the water roads where many generations of boatmen have been accustomed to tie up and stable their horses for the night. Today they are fast going the way of their great predecessors, for the motor-boat is emptying their stables and bar parlours. Though the motor travels little faster than the horse, it does not tire, so that once-familiar moorings become filled up with mud, the rings rusty from long disuse, while far into the night the boats pass by. Thanks to the survival of horse-drawn traffic on the Oxford Canal, *The Bull and Butcher* has been more fortunate than many inns we encountered subsequently. . . . It was dark and there was a thin cry of bats when we walked down to *The Bull and Butcher* after dinner. By the light of a paraffin lamp the landlord was pouring beer out of a tall enamelled jug. He was more of a farmer than a publican,

49   50   51

52

49, an octagonal toll-house on the Staffordshire and Worcestershire Canal. 50, maintenance yard and workshops on the Coventry Canal. 51, a toll-house of 1853 at Stourport on the Staffordshire and Worcestershire Canal. 52, the semi-circular porch and bay of a charming Regency lock cottage at Grindley Brook Locks on the Welsh Section of the Shropshire Union.

big-boned and swarthy, his shirt-sleeves leaving his bronzed forearms bare to the elbow. Two boat captains in dark corduroys were playing a game of five-o-one on the dartboard. Each wore a gold ring in one ear, which gleamed in the lamplight and lent them an appearance which was strangely foreign. . . ."

The Bull and Butcher has now gone the way of many other canal pubs and no longer holds a licence. Most of the canal pubs have the same pleasant Georgian character as this. A stable is almost always attached and sometimes, as at *The Cape of Good Hope* at Warwick, in days gone by the inn was also a general store where the boaters could buy food and the essentials of their craft such as tow-lines, horsewhips or

40

decorated water-cans. At important canal junctions there is almost always an inn like *The Swan* at Fradley and *The Greyhound* at Hawkesbury.

Canal cottages have their own charm and, like the bridges, are in local types with variations. They vary in date between late eighteenth century and middle nineteenth century. On the main line of the Shropshire Union there is a standard yellow brick type, probably designed by Telford himself, for with their observation bays they are very similar to a road toll-house illustrated in the *Atlas to the Life of Thomas Telford*. On the Welsh Section of the Shropshire Union, however, you will see another type of later date built by the railway company when it took over the canal—an interesting case of railway architecture to be found on the rival waterways.

Other kinds of buildings on the canals are toll-houses, often octagonal in plan, as on the Staffordshire and Worcestershire; grand brick warehouses, as at Stourport; and maintenance yards where lock-gates are made and repaired, as at Hartshill on the Coventry Canal, a late Regency affair with a clock tower.

Finally should be mentioned an important item on the list of needs of the canal constructor. This is the Stop Gate needed to isolate a particular stretch during repairs. Stop gates are set up at intervals of a few miles apart so that the water in any particular stretch between gates can be isolated and the water run off by means of pipes leading from the bottom of the canal into a nearby stream or river. The gates are similar to a single pair of lock-gates.

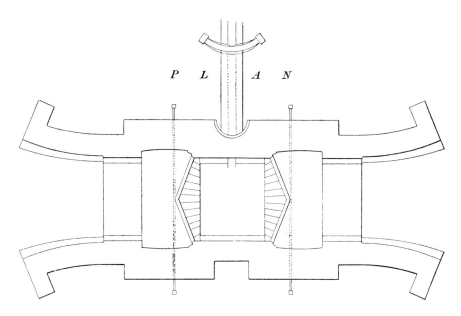

53, *engraving of the plan of a double stop gate on the Gotha Canal, which links Gothenburg with Stockholm, designed by Telford.*

54

The following pages illustrate examples of the satisfying architectural form to be found on the canals which belong to the functional tradition of design. Throughout the history of English—or for that matter of any other—architecture, there is a continuous thread running parallel with the historical styles but owing little or nothing to them. It might be called a timeless tradition of functionalism if the term had not become confused by being used to define a far more sophisticated phase of contemporary architecture. For its constituent elements are geometry unadorned, and it owes its effects to the forthright, spare and logical use of materials. To this extent it has affinities with the architectural effects sought by the architects of to-day, which no doubt explains why, looking back over the centuries, our own eyes are especially apt at picking out structures that owe their charm and quality to this tradition of functionalism, whether seen in a gothic fortress, the roof of a Wiltshire tithe-barn, a groined sea-wall, a lighthouse, a Thames-side warehouse, or one of those grand, breath-taking viaducts by which the early nineteenth century engineers carried their railways across river valleys. But the best place of all to study the functional tradition is the English canal system, perhaps because canals were mostly built at a time when the new engineering techniques aroused enough enthusiasm for pure structure to be acceptable without self-conscious adornment, and perhaps also because they perfectly combine an architectural programme with a strict engineering discipline. The architectural qualities come from a close partnership with the natural landscape and from the drama of simple geometry, with its robust and endless interplay of basic elements: steps, arches, ramps, bulging bastions and subtly concave parapet walls, all contrasted with the massive solidity of platforms and masonry retaining walls. 54, an abutment of Pontcysyllte Aqueduct. 55, (opposite) a drawbridge at Whitchurch on the Welsh Section of the Shropshire Union Canal, raised manually by a chain.

Classic arches and flowing l[i]
rising, falling, curved and strai[ght]
are the basis of the architect[ural]
quality of these canal bridges.
57, views from opposite sides of [a]
roving bridge at Aldersley Junc[tion]
where the Staffordshire and Worces[ter]-
shire Canal joins the Birming[ham]
network. 58, road bridge at St[o]

59

60

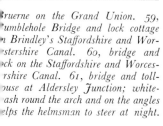

Bruerne on the Grand Union. 59, Stumblehole Bridge and lock cottage on Brindley's Staffordshire and Worcestershire Canal. 60, bridge and lock on the Staffordshire and Worcestershire Canal. 61, bridge and tollhouse at Aldersley Junction; whitewash round the arch and on the angles helps the helmsman to steer at night.

64

65

66

67

62, the brick bridge and old warehouses at Great Haywood Junction, where the Staffordshire and Worcestershire Canal joins the Trent and Mersey. The picture conveys the strange, remote, unearthly atmosphere of the old canals. 63, a general view of the same bridge. 64, Flatheridge Roving Bridge on the Staffordshire and Worcestershire. 65, an early wooden swing bridge from a print of 1806. 66, a cast iron split bridge on the Staffordshire and Worcestershire, an ingenious type which eliminates the need for taking the tow path under the bridge in that the tow rope can pass between the two cantilevered projections of the bridge. 67, the sculptural effect of a lock wall near Warwick on the Grand Union Canal.

69

Most of the Midland canal bridges are of brick, while those in the North are of stone. (Opposite) 68, a stone roving bridge south of Hyde on the Peak Forest Canal, a classic example of the functional architecture of canals. 69, a brick roving bridge at Hurleston Junction on the Shropshire Union. 70, brick bridge at Autherley Junction where the Shropshire Union joins the Staffordshire and Worcestershire.

70

Cast iron bridges. 71, a roving bridge across the cutting at the summit level of the Oxford Canal, once a tunnel and still called The Tunnel. 72, one of the standard bridges on the upper part of the Oxford Canal, built when Telford straightened out Brindley's earlier meanderings. 73, a bridge cast in 1820 between Osterley and Brentford on the Grand Union, signed "Horseley Iron Works."

71

72

73

74, a cast iron bridge signed "J Sinclair, 1837" frames a group of canal buildings comprising a disused pumping station and a lock cottage at Hawkesbury Junction where the Coventry Canal joins the Oxford. 75 a Telford bridge across the deep cutting known as The Rocket near Tyrley on the Shropshire Union. Such cuttings are typical of the later canals of Telford who preferred the straight course to the indirect winding progress of Brindley's earlier canals. These cuttings have great scenic power, largely on account of dramatic bridges like this. Sometimes several form perspective vistas, one framing another in the distance. The well-protected vegetation on the slopes is very rich—at times it is almost tropical.

74

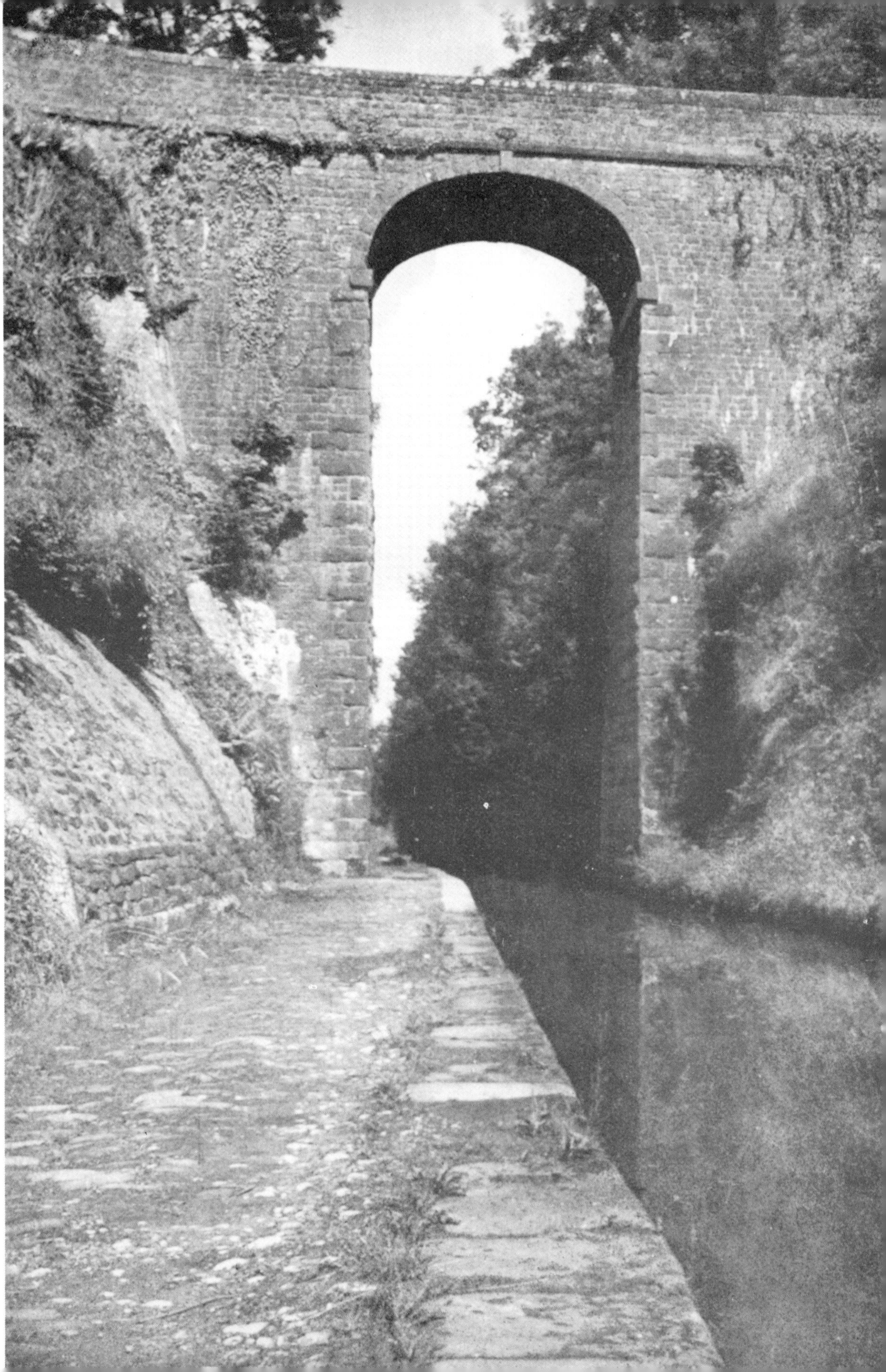

Apart from their interest as engineering feats, the canal tunnels have high dramatic
value, their squat, black openings abruptly closing the vista. 76, Shrewley Tunnel
on the Warwick and Birmingham Section of the Grand Union, 433 yards long.
77, the castellated north entrance of Sapperton Tunnel on the derelict Thames and
Severn Canal, 3,808 yards. 78, where it all began—the original entrance to the
Duke of Bridgewater's coal mine at Worsley Basin on the Bridgewater Canal.

78

77

79   80

79, entrance to the Kings Norton Tunnel on the Stratford-on-Avon Canal, 352 yards long; here boats can be hauled through by means of a handrail fixed to the side of the tunnel. 80, cutting at the Welsh end of Chirk Tunnel, 459 yards. 81, West Hill Tunnel on the Worcester and Birmingham, 2,750 yards.

81

82

83

84

85

Canal locks and bridges provide an unending series of lessons in handling that subtle but vital element of landscape design, transition from level to level. On these two pages and on the following three are a few of them—cants, cambers, ramps, steps—so defined and inter-related that they achieve something supreme in utilitarian beauty. 82, the three staircase locks at Grindley Brook on the Welsh Section of the Shropshire Union. 83, Bratch Bridge and toll-house on the Staffordshire and Worcestershire Canal. 84, 85, brick ramps at Grindley Brook. 86, lock on the Worcester and Birmingham Canal. 87, lock platform, steps and bridge, all of brick, on the Shropshire Union.

86

87

88, brick bridge and lock steps on
the Worcester and Birmingham Canal.

89

89, one of the fascinating circular lock weirs of brick found only on the Staffordshire and Worcestershire Canal. 90, richness and intricacy through wear and tear and simple, bold form add to the character of this lock on the Staffordshire and Worcestershire Canal.

90

91, one of the locks of the Bratch staircase on the Staffordshire and Worcestershire. Especially remarkable is the projecting peninsula for operating the lock gate, its line articulated by the descent of the path which mysteriously all but disappears below the bridge. 92, engraving of the plan for a lock by Telford. Though purely functional, it yet makes a fine abstract pattern.

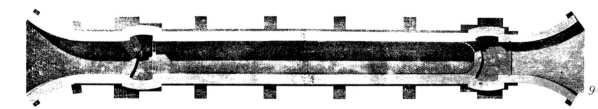

9

93, the Paddington Packet Boat, 1801.

Chapter 2: Two Hundred Years of Canals

Up to the middle of the eighteenth century people depended mainly on local agriculture and local trades. Roads were appalling, mere muddy tracks, so that all long-distance transport of goods had to be carried out by the pack-horse. But the development of the great canal system in England brought the Industrial Revolution, because it made the transport of coal from the mines to the workshops and factories a practical and paying proposition. The canals came also as a particular boon to the Potteries. Owing to heavy breakage, the transport of pottery by horse was financially crippling, but the canals brought cheap and safe carriage and also allowed easier transport of the essential raw materials of flint stones and clay.

The Bridgewater Canal opened up a new age. Though not the first English canal it was chronologically the most important and served as a pioneer and a model for the many canals which rapidly followed it. Being disappointed in love the young Duke of Bridgewater canalized his energies in the development of his estates and decided to turn to account " a large mountain of coal " which he owned at Worsley. This was quite uneconomic to mine because of the poor roads of the time and the imperfect navigation of the Mersey and the Irwell. He therefore decided to build a canal between Worsley and Manchester for which he obtained two Acts of Parliament in 1759 and 1760.

As Macpherson tells us in his *Annals of Commerce* :

" While the Duke was concerting his plans he perceived, encouraged and availed himself of the wonderful talents of the uneducated and heaven-taught engineer, Brindley, by whose ingenuity, with the abundant supply of materials from his own lands, and a vast expenditure of money for labour, he completed a navigable canal with about $4\frac{1}{2}$ ft. depth of water without locks; the inequalities of the ground, and the intervention of rivers and public roads, being surmounted by stupendous mounds of earth, by a tunnel cut through a hill 50 ft. under the surface, and in some places hewn out of the solid rock; by aqueduct bridges over

E

the public roads; and by what professional men then pronounced impossible, an aqueduct over the navigable river Irwell at the height of 38 ft. above its surface."

The canal runs right into the mines at Worsley. In Brindley's day it extended only a mile underground, but eventually, branching out in all directions, it reached to a total length of 40 miles. It is still possible to see the two entrances to the mines and the original type of mining boat used. A first-hand account of this early mine, where our canal system really began, can be found in the *Journal and Letters* of an American traveller to this country, Samuel Curwen, who records on June 7, 1777:

" With Mr. Nelson set off for the canal, intending to take a passage to Worsley to visit the Duke of Bridgewater's coal mines. After some delay we entered the passage boat, drawn by a horse in the manner of the Trek-schints in Holland. Arrived at Worsley in two hours, passing athwart the river Irwell, over which the canal runs, being raised on arches not less than fifty feet in height above that stream. In many places the bottom of the canal is considerably higher than the level of the neighbouring grounds. Sent compliments to Mr. Gilbert, the steward, asking the favour of seeing the duke's under-ground works, which was granted, and we stepped into the boat, passing into an archway partly of brick and partly cut through the stone, of about three and a half feet high; we received at entering six lighted candles. This archway, called a funnel, runs into the body of the mountain almost in a direct line three thousand feet, its medium depth beneath the surface about eighty feet; we were half an hour passing that distance. Here begins the first under-ground road to the pits, ascending into the wagon road, so called, about four feet above the water, being a highway for the wagons, containing about a ton weight of the form of a mill-hopper, running on wheels, to convey the coals to the barges or boats. Under the guidance of a minder, with each a lighted candle in his hand, we proceeded through an arched-way about five feet high, walking with our bodies at an angle of less than sixty degrees, through a road of three feet in width, a length of eight hundred yards, arrived at the coal mine, which appearing about five feet through the roof, was supported by many posts, the area being about twenty feet square and height scarce four. From this dismal abode, which my companion, whose name was Chandler, would fain have dissuaded me from proceeding to visit, after remaining a few minutes, I hastened back to our boat. One may go six miles by water in various directions, the wagon ways to the pits lying below the level of the water; it is said the distance from the mouth is six miles in the funnel. A hundred men are daily employed, and each turns out a ton a day; the miners' wages two shillings, and the laborers' about one shilling. Price of coal at the pit two pence per hundred weight; at the key threepence halfpenny, and at the door fourpence halfpenny. The boat having left, we returned to town on foot, five miles through fields and vacant lands.''

The whole canal, just over 10 miles long, was opened in 1761 after less than two years' work. To-day we have become *blasé* and are no longer stirred by such events, but at the time everyone was thrilled, especially by the Barton Aqueduct, the parent of the later splendid aqueducts of Telford and Rennie. As soon as it was proved to be effective, as Macpherson writes, even '' the scoffers, who in derision of this noble effort of Brindley's bold but unerring genius, had called it a *castle in the air*, felt themselves ashamed.'' A lady of the day describes it as '' perhaps the greatest

95, an old print of Brindley's Castle in the Air, the Barton Aqueduct, which carried the Bridge-water Canal across the River Irwell. It was replaced in 1894 by the Barton Swing Aqueduct.

artificial curiosity in the world . . . crowds of people, including those of the first fashion, resort to it daily."

Who was this astonishing character, Brindley? Samuel Smiles in his *Lives of the Engineers*, described him as " probably one of the most remarkable instances of self-taught genius to be found in the whole range of biography." Perhaps he was a type which only the age could have produced. He remained all his life almost illiterate but somehow managed to develop his gifts without any theoretical training or past experience to guide him. At an early age he was apprenticed to a millwright, the only kind of engineer that existed in those days. Later, when the Duke found him, he had set up as a wheel- and mill-wright on his own account and was carrying out much successful work, especially in flint mills for the Wedgwoods, then small potters. He died in 1772 at the early age of fifty-six, never having realized himself that it was he, as much as Wellington and Nelson, who eventually conquered Napoleon.

The Duke of Bridgewater, " the first great Manchester Man," as Smiles calls him, was no less remarkable. Though he became fabulously wealthy, at one time he gambled courageously, for during the building of his canals he had great difficulty in raising the vast sums required, even though he cut his living expenses to the minimum. At times he was even reduced to begging loans from his tenants to pay his men their wages.

In making his first canals Brindley stuck to a certain principle and method. He would lay as much of his navigation on a level as possible, and " he would rather go *round* an obstacle in the shape of an elevated range of country, than go *through* it. Although the length of canal to be worked was longer, yet the cost of tunnelling and lockage was avoided. Besides, the population of the district was fully accommodated." (Smiles.) The early canals were thus as rolling as the English roads. Later Telford and others dug their navigations in straighter lines with a greater use of cuttings and embankments.

Brindley's method of construction was to use the canal itself in forwarding the work. To quote Dr. Smiles again: " He had a floating blacksmith's forge and shop, provided with all requisite appliances, fitted up in one barge; a complete carpenter's shop in another; and a mason's shop in a third; all of which were floated on as the canal advanced, and were thus always at hand to supply the requisite facilities for prosecuting the operations with economy and despatch."

Scarcely had the first canal been opened than Brindley was at work for the Duke making an " ochilor servey or a ricconitoring " for a new " novogation " as he notes in one of his memoranda books. Soon work was proceeding on a new canal which was to join the old one at Longford Bridge and connect it with Runcorn and the Mersey, thus linking Manchester with Liverpool and the open sea. This canal was 24 miles long, on the same level of contour all the way until a flight of locks near Runcorn brought it down to the Mersey. It was opened to traffic in 1767 and later the original canal was extended north-west to Leigh.

The effect of these canals was to provide regular and abundant supplies of coal. To begin with the coal was a joy to all in the open hearth, but its full advantages were not realized until the development of Watt's steam-engine. As the Duke himself said " a navigation should always have coals at the heels of it "—a saying which still holds true.

There was considerable opposition to these early canals. They would, it was said, ruin the trade of those employed in land transport, diminish the number of draught horses, destroy great areas of cornland, wreck the coasting trade and by so doing weaken the Navy. The Jeremiahs were proved wrong, for between 1761 and 1790, when the whole country was covered with canals, the tonnage of ships leaving the English ports was nearly doubled.

During the first years after their construction, before vegetation had had time to grow, the canals must have appeared as most depressing ditches draped in mud. Miss Anna Laetitia Barbauld, writing in 1792, describes how she came to a valley where ran both a small, meandering brook and the Duke of Bridgewater's Canal.

"The firm built side of the aqueduct suddenly opened, and a gigantic form issued forth, which I soon discovered to be the *Genius of the Canal*. He was clad in a close garment of russet hue. A mural crown, indented with battlements, surrounded his brow. His naked feet were discoloured with clay. On his shoulder he bore a huge pickaxe and in his hand he held certain instruments used in surveying and levelling."

The lovely *Deity of the Stream*, however, was clothed in a light green mantle and the "clear drops fell from his dark hair, which was encircled with a wreath of water-lily, interwoven with sweet scented flag." Miss Anna would think differently to-day if she could visit the more isolated stretches of the old canals—those "broad and often beautiful roads, great highways into the heart of the most glorious country in the world," as a later writer, Temple Thurston, has described them.

As well as trading on his canals the Duke established a packet-boat service by which passengers were conveyed at the rate of a penny a mile. One of these packet-boats, the *Duchess-Countess*, still survives and languishes, the home of an old recluse, somewhere on a bank of the Welsh Section of the Shropshire Union. No doubt the Duke himself still haunts it, for (the Doctor again), "he delighted to travel by his own boats, preferring them to any more stately and aristocratic method." At the prow of the *Duchess-Countess* was fixed at one time a great S-shaped knife, which would ruthlessly cut through any tow-line which had the temerity to lie in its path, for the packet always had right of way and would travel at a good six miles an hour behind a pair of cantering horses. The larger packet-boats like the *Duchess-Countess* had accommodation for three different classes, being "each provided with a coffee house kept by the master, wherein his wife serves the company with wines and other refreshments."

96, the historic old packet boat, "Duchess-Countess," as she is to-day. The centre cabin is the only late addition to the original.

In 1766 Richard Whitworth published a treatise on *The Advantages of Inland Navigation*, in which he eulogized Brindley and the Duke, and pointed out that the development of inland navigation, instead of injuring, as had been prophesied, had greatly benefited the coasting trade and the Navy. He advocated the connection by canals of Bristol, Liverpool and Hull. Before long Brindley was at work on a scheme based on this proposal. This was the Grand Trunk Canal, Brindley's greatest enterprise. It is now known as the Trent and Mersey Canal. One of its prime movers, Josiah Wedgwood, who realized its potential advantages to the Potteries, cut the first sod in 1766, but the whole was not finished until eleven years later, after Brindley's death. The canal was to run from the Duke's Cut at Preston-on-the-Hill southwards by Northwich and Middlewich, through the great salt districts of Cheshire to the summit at Harecastle. Descending from the summit level into the

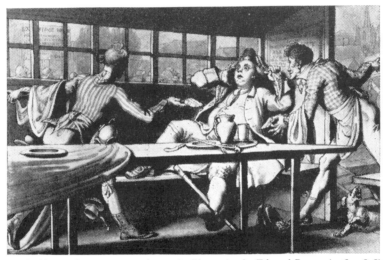

97, inside a packet, or passage, boat. An illustration by Edward Burney (1760-1848) depicting "J. Gilpin suddenly aroused by the importunities of the rival Uxbridge waiters to land and give orders for dinner." Burney was a famous book illustrator.

valley of the Trent, the canal would then pass south through the Potteries to Haywood, where it would join the projected canal to unite the Severn with the Mersey. Near Rugeley, turning north-east, it would join the Trent near Derby. From thence there was a clear navigation by Nottingham to the Humber. Another canal would be constructed named the Wolverhampton (now called the Staffordshire and Worcestershire) from the Severn to the Trent, near Haywood. In this way would be united the three rivers having their termini at the ports of Liverpool, Hull and Bristol.

The Grand Trunk itself was 140 miles long and required over 160 large and small aqueducts, 109 road bridges, 75 locks and 5 tunnels, of which by far the most formidable was the Harecastle—another of Brindley's Air Castles, as the usual gang of scoffers called it. Its manner of construction is interesting. As Smiles writes:

"Shafts were sunk from the hill-top at different points down to the level of the intended canal. The stuff was drawn out of the shafts in the usual way by horse-gins; and so long as the water was met with in but small quantities, the power of

98, a nineteenth century print of the north entrance to Harecastle Tunnels. On the right, Brindley's original tunnel; left, Telford's later tunnel with its towpath.

windmills and watermills working pumps over each shaft was sufficient to keep the excavators at work. But as the miners descended and cut through the various strata of the hill on their downward progress water was met with in vast quantities; and here Brindley's skill in pumping machinery proved of great value. . . . He had a fire-engine, or atmospheric steam-engine . . . erected on the top of the hill, by the action of which great volumes of water were pumped out night and day. This abundance of water, though it was a serious hindrance to the execution of the work, was a circumstance on which Brindley had calculated, and indeed, depended, for the supply of water for the summit level of his canal. When the shafts had been sunk to the proper line of the intended waterway, the excavation then proceeded in opposite directions, to meet the other driftways which were in progress. The work was also carried forward at both ends of the tunnel, and the whole line of excavation was at length united by a continuous driftway . . . when the water ran freely out at both ends, and the pumping apparatus on the hilltop was no longer needed."

"Gentlemen come to view our eighth wonder of the world," a contemporary notes, "the subterraneous navigation, which is cutting by the great Mr. Brindley, who handles rocks as easily as you would plum-pies, and makes the four elements subservient to his will. He is as plain a looking man as one of the boors of the Peak, or as one of his own carters; but when he speaks, all ears listen, and every mind is filled with wonder at the things he pronounces to be practicable. . . . The clay he cuts out serves for bricks to arch the subterraneous part, which we heartily wish to see finished to Wilden Ferry, when we shall be able to send Coals and Pots to London, and to different parts of the globe."

The Grand Trunk—the title was Brindley's own—became the great aorta of the Midlands canal system from which many lines developed. Brindley laid out several other canals, not all of which he completed—the Coventry, the Oxford, the Droitwich, the Chesterfield—but none surpasses the Grand Trunk in magnificence.

65

The phenomenal success of the Duke's Canal and the Grand Trunk brought the great canal boom and "the strong motive of personal gain became superadded to that of public utility." By 1792 the mania was in full swing and there was much wild speculation. Before long there was nowhere south of Durham more than 15 miles from water communication. There were many crashes but also enormous profits. Figures in the *Gentleman's Magazine* for December 1824 show that the original values of canal shares had increased on an average about thirty times.

Other canal engineers followed Brindley. One of them was the great Thomas Telford, road maker, harbour builder, architect, surveyor, designer of the Menai Bridge and would-be poet, who began life in 1757 in a shepherd's cottage in Eskdale, trained as a stonemason and was finally buried "full of years and honours" in Westminster Abbey.

His chief canal was the old Ellesmere Canal, having with its branches a total length of 112 miles. Telford's last canal was the old Birmingham and Liverpool Junction Canal (now part of the Shropshire Union) linking Brindley's Wolverhampton Canal with the Ellesmere near Nantwich via Market Drayton, and opening up a second and shorter route between Birmingham, Liverpool and Manchester. This was the last important line, excluding the Manchester Ship Canal, to be built in England. It is remarkable for the size of its earthworks and the directness of its course.

Telford also built the Caledonian Canal, the Glasgow and Ardrossan Canal, the Gloucester and Birmingham, the Macclesfield, the Gotha Canal between Gothenburg and Stockholm, constructed the second Harecastle tunnel, improved the Grand Trunk and the Birmingham, and finally shortened the northern end of the Oxford by 14 miles. Structurally his biggest innovation was the extensive use of cast iron, notably in the trough of Pontcysyllte Aqueduct and many of his bridges. On the upper part of the Oxford, for instance, you may see examples of a standard prefabricated cast-iron bridge, no doubt designed by Telford himself for they carry the towpath across Brindley's earlier windings.

Another canal man was John Rennie (1761-1821), whose most important job was the Kennet and Avon joining the River Kennet at Newbury with the River Avon at Bath, so linking London and the Thames with Bristol, which finally fulfilled a project mooted by Francis Matthew in 1655. It was pronounced at the time as one of the best executed in the Kingdom. Rennie also built the Rochdale Canal, opened in 1804 between Rochdale and Todmorden, the object of which was to open up communication between the manufacturing districts of West Yorkshire and South Lancashire to avoid the roundabout route of the Leeds and Liverpool. This is a remarkable canal for it is lifted by locks across that great ridge called the Backbone of England. Water supply proved difficult and eventually steam-engines were erected to pump back the water to summit level during the dry season. Side-ponds to act as reservoirs were also constructed to economize water. Another of Rennie's canals was the Lancaster.

The last man in the canal gallery, but not the least, was William Jessop (1745-1814) who was responsible for the famous Grand Junction. This connected the whole of the north-western navigations to London and so completed the Cross. Other work of Jessop included the Cromford and the Nottingham Canals, the Loughborough and Leicester, and the Horncastle Navigations. Jessop was also

A canal gallery. *99, Ephraim Talbot, lock-keeper at Tixall on the Staffordshire and Worcestershire Canal, who represents a colourful, individualistic eighteenth century type still to be found amongst the workers on the canals. 100, Francis, Duke of Bridgewater at the age of sixty. 101, the great James Brindley. 102, Thomas Telford.*

99

100

01

102

engaged on the Aire and Calder, the Calder and Hebble and the Trent Navigations.

By 1839, according to Rennie's calculations, 2,236 miles of improved river navigation and 2,477 miles of canals had been formed in Great Britain, in which were comprised in England and Wales some sixty-nine rivers and eighty-six canals. But the brief but vivid spell of the great Canal Age was near its end. Came in 1825 the Stockton and Darlington line, in 1830 the Liverpool and Manchester, and in 1838 the London and Birmingham. Before long it was realized that railways might pay even better than canals. Capital began to trickle and then at last to flood towards the new mania and the long, slow creeping paralysis of the canals set in. It has lasted to this day. This is not surprising, for the canals, like the railways, were primarily regarded as speculative undertakings rather than public utilities. Canal decline as a result has been a considerable national waste.

All evidence shows that the railway interest as it began to realize its power did deliberately strangle inland navigation regardless of public interest. It was the inevitable result of competitive commercialism. Though in 1846 canals such as the Oxford and Coventry were still paying dividends of 25 and 26 per cent., by then 852 miles of waterway owned by twenty-two companies had become railway property. Not always, but too often, the railway companies would, in spite of their statutory obligations to maintain their canals in navigable condition, apply subtle means of sabotage. A typical example was the banning of powered craft on all railway-owned canals when steam power was introduced. Another was the prohibition of all Sunday traffic and all night traffic, and when an ambitious scheme for the unification of the Midlands canal system was put forward in 1847 it was nullified

103, Canal Mania. A print of 1797 by Cruikshank of a canal meeting. The gentleman on the right is reading a " Report of the Engineer Respecting the Andes Canal"—typical Cruikshank humour.

104, Railway Mania. Railway promoters fight to deposit their schemes for new railways on November 30, 1845, the Board of Trade's closing date for submitting plans. Eight hundred plans were deposited at that time.

by the Birmingham Canal's falling into railway hands. By 1872 the railways had acquired 1,260 miles or nearly one-third of the waterways of England and Wales. The worst offender was always the Great Western Railway, which came to own many canals including the Kennet and Avon, the Stratford-on-Avon and the Bridgwater and Taunton. On all the Great Western navigations traffic has ceased for many years.

The canal companies were themselves partly to blame. They also were carried away by the railway mania and became too eager to realize their capital in order to embark on railway enterprise. Many of them blackmailed the railway companies into buying them out, often at extravagant prices. Moreover, before railway competition forced their reduction, canal rates were exorbitant. The canal interest never consolidated its position as did its railway rivals. The whole canal system had been built up by independent characters and groups who never learned to co-operate among themselves. Their most serious lack was a central clearing house for organizing the payment of through tolls and the speeding up of traffic by organized through routes. Nor did the canal companies ever attempt to standardize gauges, locks and equipment, to enlarge the canals or to take up carrying on their own account in a big way. Gradually the whole industry became depressed and defeated, struggling on somehow from hand to mouth. By 1905 it is recorded that over 400 miles of canal in England and Wales had become derelict or converted into railways. Perhaps the main reason why the canals have survived at all against all the odds is that at the time they were powerful they managed to secure a privileged position in the ports and have always had free access to docks, where they have paid only nominal tonnage rates.

The Legislature also failed to recognize the essential part of waterways in the national system of communications. They never received the measure of protection they deserved. A number of Select Committees and Commissions made reports from time to time but nothing was done. The most important of these was the Royal Commission, which sat between 1906 and 1910 and produced a vast mass of evidence, concluding with definite recommendations regarding the Cross. In spite of the great expense, labour and good intentions of this commission, there was no practical result, for the railway interest entrenched in the councils of the nation was too powerful.

When road transport developed, the canals were up against another strong rival. Road transport was itself a serious competitor of the railways and had the advantages that its " track " was publicly maintained and that it was more fluid, in that a car or lorry could find its way almost anywhere right up to the points of collection and delivery.

Another factor not to be overlooked, which worked against the canals, was that large scale industrialism radically altered the Trade Map of the country so that the course of many canals no longer related to modern trade routes.

In comparing waterways with road and rail it would, however, be as unfair to judge their relative merits from a survey of canals as they exist in their present outmoded and depressed condition, as it would be to compare a Brindley fire-engine with a modern electric pump. It is a curious fact, for instance, that cranes 150 years old are still operating on some canals, and that on the Bridgewater Canal the original hand pulleys are in use to-day.

105, an old print of the Paddington Canal with passage boat and warehouses.

This and the next two pages depict some typical canal folk. *106, Mr. and Mrs. John Wilson, who work their own boat "Mabel" on the Coventry and Oxford Canals. Wilson, son of a collier turned boatman, is one of the few who have bravely stood out against centralised carrying and remains one of the rare Number Ones, or owner-boatmen, left on the cut; many former Number Ones envy his independence. It is often but wrongly believed that canal boating families have gypsy blood, a belief they strongly resent. Though they have been recruited from different sources at different times, many come from English country stock originating around such canal centres as Braunston.*

107

108

109

107, Mrs. Doris Harrison of the third generation behind the bar at the old canal inn, "The Cape of Good Hope," at Warwick. 108, Jack Warner who has worked on canals all his life; now lock keeper at Tardebigge on the Worcester and Birmingham, he believes in the transmigration of souls and is famed for his songs at "Half-Way House." 109, John Moody, canal maintenance man at Ellesmere Depot on the Shropshire Union. 110, 111, 112, boaters' children. Their lives are hard but independent, and rarely are they irked and standardized by schooling; a family resemblance can be noticed amongst very many of them for there is much intermarriage among the boating families. 113, Mrs. Skinner prepares a meal in the cabin of a Narrow Boat; her husband is another of the rare Number Ones. The boat cabins measure about 7 ft. wide by 10 ft. long and all have a standard and highly functional lay-out. Decoration consists of lacework, brasses, lace-edge plates, rose and castle paintings, a minute, spotless coal range and brightly polished lock windlasses. Seated in the centre of her ædicule, curtain enshrined, children bawling vigorously around, the materfamilias of the Narrow Boat seems like some benevolent, rough-hewn goddess of fertility.

110

111

112

114, the stern fender of a Narrow Boat. 115, a Narrow Boat (sometimes called a Monkey, or Long, Boat) up on the slip for repairs at Polesworth on the Coventry Canal. Hulls are built of oak and elm, or of steel, and are flat bottomed. Timbers are caulked and dressed with a traditional concoction of tar, cow-hair and horse-dung which is applied hot and is called Chalico. 116, tea-time scene on a Narrow Boat as depicted in a drawing of 1874.

115

116

...the rudder post of a Narrow Boat decorated with geometrical design,
...t paint and pipe-clayed rope-work in nautical tradition. The entwined
...s are called Turk's Heads, the vertical piece at the stern is a Swan's
..., while the rudder post itself is known as a Ram's Head, thereby
...ps revealing an age-old link with the Long Ships of the Norsemen.

118, a white horse's tail hanging from a rudder post, a tradition decoration rarely seen to-day. The tradition began, it is said, when boating family, losing a cherished white horse, pinned its tail aste so that the beast's beauty, strength and virtue might go with them f ever. 119, roses and letters on a Narrow Boat's cabin. 120, a butt or towed boat on the Grand Union, seen from astern. 121, ga painted tillers; the far one on the butty of wood is always turn upwards at moorings; the near one on the motor boat is of steel a has its tiller extension removed. The scene is at Hawkesbury Junctio

120

121

77

Canal cottages. 122, lock cottage at Berkhamsted on the Grand Union. 123, lengthman's cottage near Audlem on the Shropshire Union, a standard type on this canal designed by Telford. 124, a bow-windowed cottage at Hawkesbury Junction where the Oxford Canal joins the Coventry; a lively watering centre.

124

123

Canal pubs. 125, " The Two Boats " at Long Itchington on the Warwick and Napton Section of the Grand Union; the walls are cream coloured stucco, the shutters and quoins are painted green. 126, " The Cross Keys " at Penkridge on the Staffordshire and Worcestershire Canal. 127, " The Greyhound " at Hawkesbury Junction. 128, " The Globe " near Leighton Buzzard on the Grand Union; its records go back 150 years and here at one time fly boats from Northampton would change horses. 129, " The Boat " at Berkhamsted with a Regency stucco front; the side drops down to the canal below. 130, " The Three Horse Shoes " at Winkwell on the Grand Union Canal, a pre-canal inn that dates from 1535.

131

131, "*The Boat*" *at Stoke Bruerne on the Grand Union.
Canal inns like this are like the posting houses of coaching
days, for here generations of boatmen have tied up and stabled
or changed their horses. The motor boat, though travelling
very little faster than the horse-drawn boat, does not tire, and
so the original purpose of these canal inns has, to a large extent,
disappeared.* 132, "*The Navigation Inn,*" *near Braunston,
on the upper part of the Oxford; on the left are the stables.*

The canal town of Stourport. This is the one complete canal town in England, having been built at the end of the eighteenth century specially as a trading and wharfage centre where the Staffordshire and Worcestershire Canal locks down to the Severn. Thereby it formed an important link between the Midlands and the sea. 133, warehouse on the main basin. 134, street scene near the main basin. 135, toll-house. 136, warehouses.

134

137, a street along the canal at Stourport, the New Town of the eighteenth century. Built complete for utilitarian and commercial purposes, it has that unselfconscious beauty of the truly functional, enhanced by the patina of age and a strange, haunted air of solitude, for with the decline of the canals Stourport lost its lively bustle. As Nash, the Worcestershire historian of the late eighteenth century, wrote: " About 1766, where the river Stour empties itself into the Severn below Mitton, stood a little alehouse called Stourmouth. Near this Brindley has caused a town to be erected, made a port and dockyards, built a new and elegant bridge, established markets and made it the wonder not only of this county but of the nation at large." Stourport has changed little since then though the old bridge has disappeared and the whole is in a sad state of neglect. The old cottages above, for instance, await demolition. What sort of soulless horror will replace their charm?

138, a Narrow Boat seen from astern on the Grand Union.

Chapter 3: The Canals Today

What is the position of canals to-day? The glossary gives detailed information, but here are some general facts and figures. With the exception of the Weaver Navigation, the Aire and Calder Navigation, the Bridgewater Canal, the Manchester Ship Canal and the Grand Union, all of which flourish, English canals remain virtually in the condition they were before the railways came. In 1905 the canals carried some 42,354,886 tons. In 1924 the figure was 16,456,000; in 1938 it was 12,952,000. Today the figure is probably not above 10,000,000, which is about 2 per cent. of all trade handled and about 3 per cent. of that handled by the railways. It has been authoritatively stated that the canals, at relatively small expense, could be made to carry 20,000,000 tons a year, or double the present traffic. The Birmingham Canal Navigations alone have a capacity of 12,000,000 tons. If the narrow boat canals, especially those contained in the busy routes of the Cross (those linking London to Liverpool and Bristol to Hull with their centre at Birmingham) were enlarged to take 100-ton boats at least, no doubt the traffic could be considerably increased above the 20,000,000 mark, to everyone's benefit. In 1941 it was calculated that there were 58 separate canals in Great Britain, of which 35 were owned by the railways and 23 by 22 independent undertakings. The mileage of these canals amounted to 2,566 miles, of which 2,118 were alleged to be open for navigation. The longest of these canals is the Grand Union with 255 miles, and the shortest, the Kensington Canal and the Duke of Marlborough's Canal between the Thames and the Oxford Canal, both of which are about $\frac{1}{2}$ mile long. The Manchester Ship Canal and the Caledonian and Crinan Canals are not included in these statements. The total mileage of broad, or barge, canals open to traffic was put at 1,278, the remaining 840 miles being available for narrow boats only. These figures are probably optimistic and are less to-day even officially, since the Huddersfield Narrow and Welshpool Section of the Shropshire Union were abandoned. Even these figures, however, show that 448 miles of canal, or $17\frac{1}{2}$ per cent. of the total mileage, have fallen into disuse

G

without being officially abandoned. The figures compiled by the 1906 Royal Commission were: 2,556 miles owned by independent companies carrying 28,168,813 tons and 1,266 owned or controlled by railways carrying 14,191,073 tons. Some of the canals are in fair working condition, others in poor condition, while some, like the valuable little Stratford-on-Avon Canal, though officially still navigable, are almost impassable owing to silting and weeds. The chief weaknesses throughout the system are shallow water caused by bank erosion, lack of standardization of works such as locks, obsolete equipment such as cranes and handling plant, inadequate wharves and depots, complete lack of amenities for the boating people and appallingly insanitary and unsightly dereliction at many industrial centres. The following glossary of canals gives some detailed information. By no means all the canals ever constructed are included, but only those which remain navigable, or if derelict or semi-derelict, deserve resuscitation. They are grouped under two headings: (1) Fully navigable. (2) Derelict, semi-derelict or unused. They are listed in alphabetical order. Rivers, unless combined with canals as part of a navigation, are not included. The figures after the word Boats show the maximum size of craft which can navigate the canal.

FULLY NAVIGABLE

AIRE and CALDER NAVIGATION. Part river, part canal. Main line: Goole Docks to Leeds Bridge near junction with Leeds and Liverpool Canal. 34 miles. 10 locks. Boats, 120 ft. by 17 ft. 6 in. Wakefield Canal: Main line canal at Castleford to junction with Calder and Hebble Navigation at Wakefield. 8 miles. 5 locks. Boats, 120 ft. by 17 ft. 6 in. Barnsley Canal: Wakefield to Barnsley. 12 miles. 15 locks. Boats, 78 ft. 6 in. by 14 ft. 6 in. Selby Canal: Main line at Knottingley to junction with River Ouse at Selby. 12 miles. 4 locks. Boats, 78 ft. 6 in. by 16 ft. 6 in. Engineers, Brindley consulted, Jessop.
remarks: Model navigation, up-to-date and efficient. Essentially a commercial waterway. Most common craft the steel compartment boat or Tom Pudding, hauled by tug in trains.

ASHBY-DE-LA-ZOUCH CANAL. Junction with Coventry Canal at Marston to Moira in Leicestershire. 30 miles. No locks. Boats, 72 ft. by 7 ft. Engineers, Jessop and Whitworth.
remarks: Some traffic in coal. Last three miles abandoned in 1943. Would make excellent pleasure canal as it passes through pleasant countryside, has no locks and is in reach of areas of dense population. Ware made at Measham at one time, together with brasswork and painted objects has been among the traditional appurtenances of the boatman's cabin. The ware is a brown salt glaze stoneware with embossed and coloured decorations.

BIRMINGHAM CANAL NAVIGATION. Birmingham is the centre of the canal system of England; canals in and around it form a complex network 160 miles in extent. Main tracks: (1) Main Line: Worcester Bar, Birmingham junction with Worcester and Birmingham Canal to junction with Staffs. and Worcs. Canal at Aldersley. 15½ miles. 24 locks. (2) Birmingham and Fazeley Canal: Junction with main line near Worcester Bar to junction with Coventry Canal at Fazeley and with detached part of same canal at Whittington Brook. 15 miles. 38 locks. Along its route has two important junctions with Grand Union Canal. (3) Wyrley and Essington Canal: Horseley Fields Junction with main line to junction with detached part of Coventry Canal at Huddlesford. 24 miles. 30 locks. Little used and weedy. (4) Dudley Canal: Junction with old Main Loop Line to junction with Stourbridge Canal leading to Staffs. and Worcs. Canal at Stourton Bridge. 5 miles. 12 locks. Little used and weedy; parts closed.

remarks: The whole system takes narrow boats only, 70 ft. by 7 ft.

BRIDGEWATER CANAL. Junction with Rochdale Canal at Castlefield, Manchester to junctions with Manchester Ship Canal at Manchester and Runcorn and Trent and Mersey Canal at Preston Brook. Three branches including one with Weaver Navigation. Manchester to Runcorn, 28 miles. Preston Brook to Trent and Mersey, 24 miles. Locks at Runcorn and Manchester. Boats, 70 ft. by 14 ft. 9 in. Engineer, Brindley.

remarks: In good condition. Container loading used on the boats on this canal— a principle which should be widely adopted. Notable for Barton Swing Aqueduct and for its history in being first canal of Canal Era. At Worsley Basin can still be seen entrances to Duke of Bridgewater's colliery and original colliery boats.

CALDER and HEBBLE NAVIGATION. Junction with Aire and Calder at Wakefield to junction with Rochdale Canal at Sowerby Bridge. 21½ miles. 39 locks. Boats, 57 ft. 6 in. by 14 ft. 2 in. Engineer, Smeaton.

remarks: Considerable part consists of original course of river. At one time one of most prosperous of waterways. Provides link between Humber ports and Manchester and Liverpool, and serves number of busy manufacturing towns of West Riding. Fairly busy and essentially a commercial waterway.

COVENTRY CANAL. Junction with Oxford Canal at Hawkesbury Junction to junction with Trent and Mersey at Fradley. Has junction with Birmingham and Fazeley Canal at Fazeley and for about 5 miles continues as Birmingham and Fazeley Canal, detached part of Coventry starting again at Whittington Brook— typical instance of past organizational confusion. Hawkesbury to Fradley, 32½ miles. Coventry Basin to Fazeley, 27 miles. Hawkesbury to Coventry, 5½ miles. Detached part from Whittington to Trent and Mersey, 5½ miles. 14 locks. Boats, 71 ft. 9 in. by 7 ft. Engineer, begun by Brindley.

remarks: The Coventry, Ashby-de-la Zouch and Oxford conjointly provide longest canal level in England—51 miles—discounting the stop-lock at Hawkesbury.

EXETER SHIP CANAL. Turf Lock, River Exe Estuary to Exeter. 5½ miles. Two alternative tidal lock entrances—Turf lock taking boats 120 ft. by 26 ft. by 11 ft. 6 in. draught, and Topsham Lock taking boats 88 ft. by 25 ft.

remarks: Present canal built under Telford following an Act of 1829, but as early as 1563 in Elizabeth's reign a ship canal was built here by John Trew to take boats with draughts up to 9 ft. It was, in fact, the first English pound-lock canal. Not busy at present time.

GLOUCESTER and SHARPNESS SHIP CANAL. Entered from Bristol Channel through Sharpness Docks to junction with Severn at Gloucester. 16 miles. Entrance locks at Sharpness and a lock connecting Severn with Gloucester. Boats, 250 ft. by 30 ft. by 13 ft. draught. Engineer, Telford.

G*

remarks: Formerly called Gloucester and Berkeley Ship Canal. Constructed to avoid dangerous reaches of Severn between Sharpness and Gloucester. Fair condition and fairly busy.

GRAND UNION CANAL. Main Line: Junction with Thames at Brentford to Norton Junction. 89 miles. 96 locks. Boats, 72 ft. by 14 ft. 3 in. At Norton it divides: (1) To junction with Birmingham Canal Navigations at Birmingham. 48 miles. 63 locks. Boats, 72 ft. by 14 ft. 3 in. On this route Oxford Canal shares same waterway between Braunston and Napton. (2) To Leicester, Loughborough, junction

139, the entrance to the Regent's Canal at Limehouse from a Shepherd drawing.

with River Trent at Trent Junction, Long Eaton, thence to Langley Mill and junction with Cromford Canal. 78 miles. 73 locks. Boats, 72 ft. by 14 ft. 3 in. Main line branches: (i) Regent's Canal: Limehouse to Paddington Basin. 8½ miles. 13 locks. Boats 78 ft. by 14 ft. 6 in. (ii) Hertford Union Canal: Junction with Regent's Canal at Bethnal Green to Old Ford Junction with River Lea. 3 miles. 3 locks. Boats, 72 ft. by 14 ft. 3 in. (iii) Paddington Arm: Paddington Basin to Bulls Bridge Junction on main line. 13½ miles level. There are several other arms, notably Slough, Wendover, Aylesbury, Northampton, Market Harborough, and Buckingham.

remarks: Most of the locks throughout are 14 ft. 3 in. wide except on the upper arms which are narrow. The navigations throughout are mostly used by narrow boats, although up to Berkhamsted broad boats are seen. The Grand Union was formed by the amalgamation in 1929 of nine canals, including the Grand Junction, and is now the longest canal in England. Main line notable for its long tunnels at Braunston and Blisworth. Being an arm of the Cross it is a busy commercial route and not ideal for pleasure boating. It also has an average of one wide lock per mile which is heavy work for pleasure. The Wendover, Aylesbury and Market Harborough Arms are little used today. John Nash gave a good example to town planners by co-operating with the promoters of the Regent's Canal and so including a stretch of it picturesquely in his park.

86

HUDDERSFIELD BROAD CANAL. From junction with main line of Calder and Hebble Navigation at Cooper Bridge with Huddersfield Narrow Canal at Huddersfield. 4 miles. 9 locks. Boats, 57 ft. 6 in. by 14 ft. 2 in. by 4 ft. 6 in. draught.

remarks: Formerly called Sir John Ramsden's Canal, as Ramsden, who owned most of Huddersfield at one time, obtained an Act for its execution in 1774. Later Ramsden extended the canal south-west as the Huddersfield Narrow Canal. In fair condition. The locks on the Calder and Hebble upper part, as well as those on the Huddersfield Broad, cannot pass craft more than 57 ft. 6 in. long. This means that Leeds and Liverpool Canal boats (up to 62 ft.) cannot work through to this section— an anomaly which should be removed in any future canal programme.

LEEDS and LIVERPOOL CANAL. Liverpool to junction with Aire and Calder Navigation at Leeds. 127 miles. 92 locks. Boats, 61 ft. by 14 ft. 4 in. Two important branches: (1) Rufford Branch to junction with River Ribble Estuary. 7 miles. 8 locks. (2) Leigh Branch from Wigan to north end of Bridgewater Canal. 7 miles. 4 locks. Engineer, Brindley but Whitworth continued the work.

remarks: Important canal. In fair condition but not busy at present time. Numerous swing bridges slow traffic and should be replaced by overbridges. Leeds and Liverpool short boats navigate canal and branches. Rises 500 ft. over Pennines. A gigantic undertaking requiring forty-six years to complete. Notable feature is Five-Rise Lock at Bingley and also the great Burnley Embankment. Section between Bingley and Foulridge a delightful pleasure cruising ground.

MANCHESTER SHIP CANAL. Eastham Locks at junction with Mersey to Docks, Manchester. 36 miles. 5 locks. Used by vessels up to 15,000 tons of maximum size 600 ft. by 65 ft. Engineer, Sir E. Leader Williams.

remarks: The last great canal enterprise in England, being opened in 1894. By connecting Manchester to the sea has brought great benefit to trade and remains a busy waterway. Notable for the Barton Swing Aqueduct carrying Bridgewater Canal. Essentially commercial but pleasure boats are permitted to use it.

OXFORD CANAL. Junction with Thames at Oxford to junction with Coventry Canal at Hawkesbury. Has junction with Grand Union at Napton Junction and shares same waterway from there to Braunston. 78 miles. 46 locks. Boats, 70 ft. by 7 ft. as far as Napton, thereafter 70 ft. by 14 ft. Engineer, Brindley.

remarks: Important canal and one of few which was still paying dividend up to year of nationalisation. Most of traffic occurs at north part between Napton and Hawkesbury. In fair condition. Passes through remote and beautiful countryside and is eminently suitable for long-distance pleasure craft. Features of interest: early cast-iron bridges between Braunston and Hawkesbury and wooden drawbridges on southern part peculiar to Oxford Canal. Canal company's Regency office building in Oxford at end of canal basin and fine early warehouse by this basin are notable. This basin site has been sold to Lord Nuffield.

SHEFFIELD and SOUTH YORKSHIRE NAVIGATION. Junction with River Trent at Keadby near Scunthorpe to Sheffield. 43 miles. 31 locks. Boats, 61 ft. 6 in. by 15 ft. 6 in.

remarks: In first-class condition with heavy traffic. Essentially commercial waterway.

SHROPSHIRE UNION CANAL, MAIN LINE. Autherley Junction near Wolverhampton, where it links with Staffs. and Worcs. Canal, to Ellesmere Port, junction with Manchester Ship Canal. 66½ miles. 49 locks. Boats, 72 ft. by 6 ft. 11 in. from Autherley to Bunbury, 71 ft. 9 in. by 13 ft. 2 in. from Bunbury to Ellesmere Port. Apart from Welsh Section there are two branches: (1) Middlewich Branch connecting with Trent and Mersey Canal. 10 miles. 3 locks. Boats, 75 ft. by 6 ft. 10 in. (2) Shrewsbury or Norbury Branch from Norbury to Withington near Shrewsbury. 17 miles. 25 locks. Boats, 74 ft. by 6 ft. 4 in. Middlewich Branch is still open to traffic but Shrewsbury Branch is now derelict. Engineer, Telford.

remarks: Both main line and Shrewsbury Branch are excellent for pleasure traffic. They pass through fine landscape and the main line has a level from Autherley to Tyrley of 25 miles with only one lock. The Shrewsbury Branch should be revived for pleasure. The main line, originally called the Birmingham and Liverpool

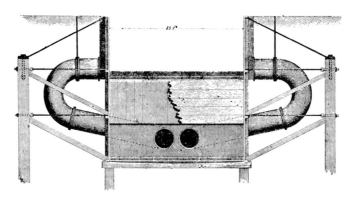

140, section through a cast-iron lock designed by Telford for the Ellesmere and Chester Canal.

Junction Canal, was the last of the big canals and was built to form a shorter and easier route from the Midlands to the North in reply to the railway threat. It is the straightest of canals with splendid cuttings and embankments and is in marked contrast to the earlier winding canals of Brindley. Many fine bridges. Still a fair trade on main line but it is badly silted. Known colloquially as the Shroppie Cut.

STAFFORDSHIRE and WORCESTERSHIRE CANAL. Junction with Severn at Stourport to junction with Trent and Mersey Canal at Great Haywood. 50 miles. 52 locks. Boats, 72 ft. by 7 ft. Engineer, Brindley.

remarks: At one time trade on this canal was immense and between Stourport, Wolverhampton and Gailey Wharf near Cannock Collieries there has been considerable traffic in coal, mostly by day boats. From Gailey Wharf to Great Haywood it is virtually disused. At Compton near Wolverhampton can be seen Brindley's first lock. The canal is beautiful for most of its length and is characterized by its rocky cuttings. It was originally called the Wolverhampton Canal and is colloquially known as the Stour Cut. Contains many pleasant brick bridges and canal cottages, bridges being unique in having cast-iron plaques bearing name and number. Also contains the rare cast-iron split bridges at its southern end. Stourport, where the canal begins, was built specifically as a waterway centre—the one complete canal town in England; of great fascination with its old warehouses and Georgian streets; could be revitalized as tourist centre for the Midlands.

STOURBRIDGE CANAL. Junction with Staffs. and Worcs. Canal at Stewponey via Stourbridge to Birmingham Canal at Black Delph, Brierley Hill. 8 miles. 20 locks. Boats, 70 ft. by 7 ft.
remarks: Still used to a minor extent. Forms useful alternative route to Birmingham from the Staffs. and Worcs. Canal.

TRENT and MERSEY CANAL. Derwent Mouth, River Trent, to Preston Brook, junction with Bridgewater Canal. 93½ miles. 117 locks. Boats, 70 ft. by 7 ft. Engineer, Brindley.
remarks: One of three main cross-country canals. Connects with Derby, Coventry, Staffordshire and Worcestershire Canal, Macclesfield Canal, Shropshire Union Canal and River Weaver. It is in fact the old Grand Trunk. Notable features are the Harecastle Tunnels and the Anderton Lift connecting the canal with the River Weaver. Still busy in north part. In fair condition but in great need of dredging.

WORCESTER and BIRMINGHAM CANAL. Junction with Severn at Worcester to junction with Birmingham Canal Navigations at Worcester Bar, Birmingham. 30 miles. 58 locks. Boats, 70 ft. by 7 ft.
remarks: The canal is still used but to a limited extent. Should be revitalized as important link between Birmingham and the Severn. Also has great possibilities for pleasure boating with a 15-mile level stretch from Birmingham. Notable for flight of 30 locks at Tardebigge.

DERELICT, SEMI-DERELICT OR UNUSED CANALS

ASHTON CANAL. Junction with Rochdale Canal at Manchester to junction with Huddersfield Narrow Canal and with Peak Forest Canal at Ashton-under-Lyne. Main canal, 6½ miles. Four branches, 10 miles in all. Locks: main canal, 18; Hollinwood Branch, 7; others, none. Boats, 70 ft. by 7 ft.
remarks: Should be revived to form useful through-route for pleasure boating to the Peak Forest and Macclesfield Canals. Potentially a valuable commercial waterway for Manchester traffic.

BASINGSTOKE CANAL. Junction with River Wey near Byfleet through Woking and Aldershot to Basingstoke. 37 miles. 29 locks. Boats, 72 ft. by 14 ft.
remarks: Semi-derelict but lower section still sometimes used. Tunnel at Greywell impassable. One of few canals not nationalized. Very suitable for pleasure boating as it connects with the Thames via the Wey, and has beautiful stretches with a long summit level of 20 miles. Mr. J. F. Pownall has prepared an excellent scheme which would join the canal to the Kennet and Avon Canal above Newbury, giving a single pound 40 miles long. The canal would then act as a through route for navigation and also as a local water distributor giving underground storage in the Bagshot hills for use by the Metropolitan Water Board, as an alternative to the Enborne reservoir scheme. The proposal would give a broad boat route between London and Bristol 20 miles shorter than the present one via the Thames and the Kennet and Avon as it would cut out the Thames windings. Estimated cost: £1,712,000.

CHESTERFIELD CANAL. Junction with River Trent at Stockwith to Shireoak Basin. 28 miles. 24 locks. Boats, 72 ft. by 6 ft. 10½ in. Engineers, begun by Brindley and completed by his brother-in-law, Henshall.

remarks: Canal between Shireoak Basin and Chesterfield, not now navigable, of a length of 45 miles containing 41 locks. Should be opened its entire length for pleasure boating.

CROMFORD CANAL. Junction with Grand Union Canal at Langley Mill to Cromford. 12½ miles with 2 mile Pinxton Branch. 14 locks. Boats, 78 ft. by 7 ft. (6 ft. 9 in. Pinxton Branch). Engineer, Jessop.

remarks: Has summit level of 14 miles dug deeper than the rest to act as reservoir. Interesting aqueduct at Derwent, 200 yds. long by 30 ft. high.

DERBY CANAL. Junction with Grand Union Canal at Sandiacre to junction with Trent and Mersey Canal at Swarkestone. 14½ miles. 9 locks. Boats, 72 ft. by 14 ft.

remarks: Has been disused for some time, though not yet officially abandoned. One of the few un-nationalized canals. Should be re-opened for general traffic. Would be specially useful to the Derby Gas Light and Coke undertaking.

DROITWICH CANAL. Links Droitwich with the Severn. 6 miles. 8 locks. Boats, 71 ft. 6 in. by 14 ft. 6 in. Engineer, Brindley.

remarks: Should be reopened for pleasure traffic and used in conjunction with the:

DROITWICH JUNCTION CANAL. Links Droitwich with the Worcester and Birmingham Canal. 1½ miles. 6 locks. Boats, 71 ft. 6 in. by 7 ft. 1 in.

remarks: Should be reopened for general traffic both for pleasure and local commerce. Now completely derelict.

FOSSDYKE CANAL. Junction with River Trent at Torksey to junction with River Witham at High Bridge, Lincoln. 11 miles. One double lock at Torksey. Boats, 74 ft. by 15 ft. 2 in.

remarks: Originally built by the Romans for the conveyance of corn. The oldest artificial waterway in the country still navigable at the present time. Scoured out by Henry I in 1121. Little used today. Should be used for pleasure and preserved as an ancient monument.

HUDDERSFIELD NARROW CANAL. Junction with Huddersfield Broad Canal at Huddersfield to junction with the Ashton Canal at Ashton-under-Lyne. 19 miles. 74 locks. Boats, 70 ft. by 6 ft. 11 in.

remarks: Abandoned in 1944. No longer open for general traffic but pleasure boats may use it under permit. About forty men are now employed full time in maintaining this abandoned waterway of 19 miles, yet it is in a very poor condition—a typical example of present canal morale. The canal reaches the highest summit level in England at 638 ft. and contains the longest tunnel—the Standedge, 3 miles 135 yds. long. An Inland Waterways Association Report states: " Standedge Tunnel, though of very restricted bore, is a most impressive work, bearing in mind the time of its construction. Railway tunnels run parallel with the canal upon each side but at a slightly higher level The canal tunnel drains the railway tunnels and assists in ventilation. It was evidently utilized in the construction of the railway tunnels, and all the tunnels are interlinked by communicating galleries. The canal tunnel widens in places to an extent sufficient to enable boats to pass each other.

We considered the tunnel not incapable of exploitation as a revenue-producing tourist attraction, especially as a main line railway station adjoins each end readily reached from the many dense conurbations of the area. Passing largely through the natural rock, the bore bears some resemblance to such major sights as the Speedwell Mine in the Peak District; and its position as the longest canal tunnel and on the highest canal level is an added attraction. Right to navigate the tunnel with tourist parties might perhaps be hired out to some small contractor of enterprise."

KENNET and AVON NAVIGATION. Junction with the Thames at Reading to junction with River Avon (Bristol) at Hanham. 86 miles. 106 locks. Boats, 73 ft. by 13 ft. 10 in. Engineer, Rennie.

remarks: The navigation consists of the River Kennet Navigation, Kennet and Avon Canal and River Avon Navigation and links the Thames with the Bristol Channel. At one time an extremely important navigation, but it came into the hands of the Great Western Railway and is now semi-derelict and not used by commercial boats. Passage is barely possible even for small pleasure craft. Even since nationalization the passage of boats has, for unknown reasons, been discouraged—a quite unwarranted state of affairs, considering the number of men employed in maintenance. Should at once be revived, as it must in any case remain open for drainage purposes. An architectural feature is the fine Dundas Aqueduct over the River Avon 6 miles from Bath. Another feature of interest is the long flight of 29 locks, with their large side ponds at Devizes.

LANCASTER CANAL. Preston to Lancaster (including branch to Glasson), and Lancaster to Kendal. 60 miles. Locks: main canal, 8; Glasson Branch, 7. Boats, 72 ft. by 14 ft. 6 in. Engineers, Brindley and Whitworth surveyed the canal but it was completed by Rennie.

remarks: At one time it was linked by a special railway to the Leeds and Liverpool Canal, but is now isolated. It is used very little and was threatened with abandonment in 1943, but escaped through the action of the Kendal Municipality. A very important canal in its time and one which established Rennie's reputation. A regular passenger boat service runs on this canal during the summer months which should serve as a model for other waterways. The canal should be maintained for pleasure and local trading as it passes through fine scenery with extensive sea and mountain views. It is perhaps only second in beauty to the Welsh Section of the Shropshire Union. The Lancaster Aqueduct built to carry the canal over the River Lune in 1796 is a notable feature.

MACCLESFIELD CANAL. Junction with Peak Forest Canal at Marple to junction with Trent and Mersey Canal at Hall Green. 26 miles. 13 locks. Boats, 70 ft. by 7 ft. Engineer, Telford.

remarks: One of the later canals. Built to shorten the distance between London and Manchester by 13 miles. In poor condition, but should be revived with the Ashton and Peak Forest Canals for general purposes.

MIDDLE LEVEL NAVIGATIONS. Network of waterways lying between and connecting River Nene with River Ouse such as King's Dike, Pophams Eau, Well Creek and many others. Main line from River Nene at Peterborough to Great Ouse at Salters Lode Sluice, 30 miles. Maximum size of boats using main line, 46 ft. by 11 ft.

remarks: All the waterways are artificial cuts or old improved streams intended mainly for drainage of the Fens but also for local agricultural transport. Most are in poor condition, choked with weeds and rubbish. Main navigation at least should be scoured out as it is the only link between the Fenlands, the Nene and the general canal system.

PEAK FOREST CANAL. Junction with Ashton Canal at Dukinfield to Bugsworth. $14\frac{1}{2}$ miles. 16 locks. Boats, 70 ft. by 7 ft. Engineer, Outram.

remarks: Not very successful until it was connected with the Macclesfield Canal, when it became one of the lines connecting Manchester with London and the midland counties. The Ashton, Macclesfield and Peak Forest Canals may be considered as a unit, forming a through route between the Potteries and Manchester. Now there is no regular commercial traffic on this line and the general condition is poor. In parts the landscape is grand and mountainous. The three canals should be among the first to be revived for pleasure traffic. A notable feature is Cotton-king Oldknow's monumental aqueduct at Marple.

ROCHDALE CANAL. Junction with Calder and Hebble Navigation at Sowerby Bridge to junction with Ashton Canal and Bridgewater Canal at Manchester. 33 miles. 83 locks. Boats, 74 ft. by 14 ft. 1 in. Engineer, Rennie.

remarks: There is now very little through traffic and the canal is under threat of abandonment. It is badly silted and in a derelict condition throughout. It is, however, a valuable connecting link between the Mersey and the Humber by providing a broad boat navigation between the Calder and Hebble and Manchester. It should be revived and modernized. It was a great engineering achievement for its time. Not perhaps of greatest value for pleasure owing to the heavy lockage, though its scenery is magnificent.

141, an aquatint of 1793, from Boydell's " History of the River Thames," showing the junction of the Thames with the and Severn Canal at Inglesham. In the distance is the spire of Lechlade Church. The round cottage is typical of this*

SHREWSBURY or NORBURY CANAL. See section on the Shropshire Union Canal, Main Line.

SHROPSHIRE UNION CANAL, WELSH SECTION. (1) Llantisilio Branch: Junction with main line at Hurleston to Llantisilio. 36 miles. 21 locks. Boats, 72 ft. by 6 ft. 10 in. Engineer, Telford.

remarks: Abandoned for general traffic, but as it acts as a feeder from the Dee to the main line it must be kept open. It is still navigable by pleasure craft, but almost impassable at points owing to silting and weeds. Passes across the famous aqueducts of Chirk and Pontcysyllte and through fine scenery including the Vale of Llangollen. Perhaps the most lovely of all canals. Should definitely be reconditioned for pleasure boating and perhaps placed under control of the National Trust. At present the many fine little bridges across the canal are threatened with destruction by local authorities. This branch could, incidentally, be very useful for the transport of peat from Wixhall Moss.

(2) Newtown Branch: Frankton Junction near Ellesmere, where it joins the Llantisilio Branch, to Newtown. 35 miles. 26 locks. Boats, 72 ft. by 6 ft. 10 in.

remarks: Formerly known as the Montgomery Canal. Now completely derelict and abandoned in 1944, some parts of it being piped. This is the result of a breach which occurred in 1934. It was not a serious matter to repair, but the opportunity was taken later to abandon it. This branch should be reopened for pleasure as a major tourist attraction as its scenery is very fine. It is interesting to note that the original intention was to construct the main line from Shrewsbury from a junction with the Severn up, via Frankton and Pontcysyllte, to Chester, the line from Pontcysyllte being merely an intake branch. That is why the grand Pontcysyllte Aqueduct was built. As the canal was eventually laid out the aqueduct is not really necessary, as the intake branch could have proceeded up the Vale of Llangollen on the south side.

STRATFORD-ON-AVON CANAL. Stratford-on-Avon to junction with the Worcester and Birmingham Canal at King's Norton. 25½ miles. 56 locks. Boats, 71 ft. by 7 ft.

remarks: There is a junction half-way at Kingswood with the Grand Union Canal. Having once belonged to the Great Western Railway, the canal is in an appalling condition, and though still officially navigable it is almost impassable owing to the thick duck-weed which covers it from end to end, and the decrepit state of the locks. No trading boat has used this canal for the past eleven years, though an occasional intrepid pleasure boat will sometimes force a passage; in such a case the officials are compelled to assist and do so by clearing a passage with an icebreaker and temporarily lifting a fixed bridge obstruction (once a drawbridge) near King's Norton*. There is every reason why this canal should be revived, for it would make an important alternative route south of Birmingham and also a short cut on to the Worcester and Birmingham Canal, besides providing a delightful pleasure resort for Birmingham and Stratford people. A notable feature is the rare type of Guillotine Lock at King's Norton Junction.

STROUDWATER CANAL. Junction with the Severn at Framilode to Wallbridge near Stroud, where it joins the defunct Thames and Severn Canal. 8 miles. 13 locks. Boats, 70 ft. by 15 ft. 6 in.

remarks: Virtually disused. Should be revived in conjunction with the:

* At the time of going to press good news comes that the fixed bridge has been replaced by a new drawbridge.

THAMES and SEVERN CANAL. Wallbridge near Stroud, where it joins the Stroudwater Canal, to the Thames at Inglesham. 29 miles. 44 locks. Boats, 70 ft. by 11 ft. Engineer, Whitworth.

remarks: Never a very successful canal owing to the competition of the shorter route between Bristol and London by the Kennet and Avon, and also to leakage troubles. Another major piece of wreckage by the Great Western Railway as it is now completely derelict. In 1901 the Gloucestershire County Council took over the canal and made an unsuccessful attempt to reopen it. The last man to navigate it must have been Temple Thurston who describes his journey along it in 1911 in his book *The Flower of Gloster*. Notable for the Sapperton Tunnel, second longest in England, for its circular, tower-like canal cottages and for the fine country, including the Golden Valley, through which it passes. The only Cotswold canal, its revival should be considered. It was at one time linked to the Kennet and Avon by the Wilts and Berks Canal, long since defunct.

WEY and ARUN NAVIGATION. Junction with the River Wey between Guildford and Godalming to junction with the River Arun. 18 miles.

remarks: Was built late and abandoned early but formed a good link between the Thames and Arundel on the south coast, and with the Portsmouth and Arundel Canal, it created a link between London and Portsmouth. Now completely derelict. There is probably little hope of its ever being revived, though amateur yachtsmen must sigh for its passing.

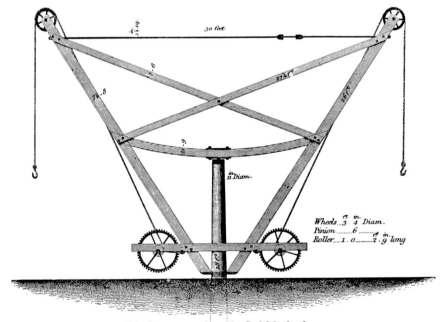

This Crane was used on the Rochdale Canal.

142, engraving from the " Atlas to the Life of Thomas Telford".

143

The railway line, beginning as an alien intruder into the peace of the English countryside, is now so characteristic a part of it that no pastoral scene is complete without a plume of smoke traversing the middle distance. In the same way the canals now take a natural place in the rural land-scape. Even their mechanical equipment, completely functional in origin, can now be regarded as a series of objects that exist in their own right. They have established themselves as surely as the church spire, the wind-mill on the hill and the signal box at the level-crossing. Many of them have considerable sculptural power and give us what may be termed Sculpture by Accident. Some typical specimens are illustrated on these pages with emphasis on the background against which they are always seen; the hard metallic silhouette of sluice machinery against still water and grassy banks with distant views of canal-side pub or lock-keeper's cottage; the heavy timber beams and railings of lock gates against a varied pattern of paving and pathways—pathways that are themselves disposed into sculptural shapes when they climb on to the upper platform of the lock and down the other side to join the towpath; finally curbs, capstans and bollards, weather-worn and grooved by friction, demonstrating that time can mellow functional objects without depriving them of the elemental vigour of their form. 143, cast iron bollard at Stoke Bruerne. 144, a wooden bollard.

144

145, a pattern of textures and forms at Hackgreen Lock on the Shropshire Union; o
the left an iron curb to protect the brickwork of the bridge from rubbing tow lines; i
time the lines form deep notches in the iron. 146, lock paddle, or sluice valve, at Hatto
on the Warwick and Birmingham Section of the Grand Union. The Hatton lock
were rebuilt in 1932, and all contain these modern paddles with their gearing enclose
in a protective metal casing. In the distance is a flight of locks known by the prosaic a
" The Thick of Hatton " and by the poetic as " The Golden Steps to Heaven." A
locks on canals are worked by the boat crews and are usually prepared in advance of
boat by a so-called Lock Wheeler, who goes ahead along the towpath on a bicycle

147

Accidental Sculpture in cast iron. 147, *lock paddle and balance beam at Hurleston Junction on the Shropshire Union; in the background is a length-man's cottage—an example of railway architecture on the canals, as it was built by the Shropshire Union Railways and Canal Company.* 148, *the guillotine or portcullis stop lock at Kings Norton Junction, where the Stratford-on-Avon Canal joins the Worcester and Birmingham, a fine piece of early cast iron engineering—a sculptural mobile.* 149, *cast iron rack and pinion paddle gearing at Tardebigge on the Worcester and Birmingham Canal.* 150, *lock gearing at Tardebigge; in the distance is the fine spire of Tardebigge Church, built in the late eighteenth century to designs by Hiorn of Warwick.* 151, *a scene on the Worcester and Birmingham near "The Half-Way House."* 152, *gears of an early crane at Ellesmere.*

148

151

152

99

Most impressive as pieces of accidental sculpture on the canals are the bollards used for tying up boats at locks or moorings. Those of wood, formed originally into firm geometric shapes by the craftsmen, in time acquire added attractions of texture and fantastic form by long use and the weather. Those of iron, by contrast, retain their clean pristine shapes, except for the pattern of grooves created by decades of

157

be friction. *153, a tall and rugged post at Hawkesbury Junction. 154, an ageing but robust cast iron bulb* *Hawkesbury Junction with a collar worn by lines which have manœuvred boats round a sharp* *nd through several generations. 155, 156, two cast iron types. 157, a graven image on the Coventry.*

Lock balance beams project from lock gates, balance their weight and act as levers. They are mostly of great solid pieces of timber but sometimes nowadays of steel weighted with concrete. Time gives the timber beams impressive textures. 158, the stop-lock at Marston Junction where the Coventry joins the Ashby.

159, Bridgewater Halfpenny Token of 1793.

Chapter 4: Have the Canals a Future?

The amount of traffic that can be carried by water in this country is, of course, limited, but by no means insignificant. In the national interest inland navigation should now be developed to its full extent. The following are the chief advantages of water transport from a purely commercial point of view:

(1) The cost of transport is less on water than on road and rail. Maintenance and running costs are low because the wear and tear of materials, due to friction, are slight. It has been estimated that the cost of maintaining the track, works and vehicles is four and a half times more on railways than on waterways. Capital costs are also far lower. While the average railway truck weighs half or three-quarters as much as its load, a canal boat or barge weighs about a fifth of its load. Compared with lorries, boats cost less to build and last longer.

(2) It is more economical to carry goods when the unit of conveyance is large. This advantage is greater on water because there the ratio of expenses diminishes in proportion as the load increases to a greater extent than on rail or road. In boats travelling at low speeds, water resistance increases very little with increase of load.

(3) In theory road and rail transport are far speedier than water transport, but for certain types of non-perishable goods such as coal, sand, concrete, petroleum products, manure, feeding stuffs, bricks, timber, grain and flour, where there is a steady replenishment of standing stocks, speed is less essential than a steady flow. Moreover, speed is of less importance in small countries like England where distances are relatively short. In practice, speed of delivery by boat is often more rapid than by rail owing to the congestion at rail depots. For heavy machinery and for fragile articles such as pottery and glass water transport is especially suitable.

(4) Like road transport, but unlike rail, water transport can load or unload almost anywhere along the route.

(5) An average waterway can safely accommodate a larger amount of traffic than an average railway, and boats can follow or pass each other closely.

Secondary Functions of Waterways

Apart from their value for cheap commercial transport, the waterways have other uses: (1) For holidays and pleasure. This is important to certain Imponderables, such as health and happiness, which cannot be measured in financial terms. But even here the commercial mind can take heart for, if properly organized to do so, the waterways could bring considerable profits from pleasure boating alone, both

I

from those who prefer uncongested holiday resorts and from foreign visitors who wish to see the country from a new and exceptionally attractive angle. The extraordinary success of the Norfolk Broads for pleasure boating provides a precedent. (2) For visual and scenic amenity. This function is linked with the first and again cannot be considered commercially. How delightful the canals could be as a landscape feature is suggested in the concluding pages of this treatise. (3) Waterways are part and parcel of the natural structure and ecology of the country and both canals and rivers are important agents of water supply, conservation and drainage. They also assist crop irrigation and the watering of cattle.* Therefore, where a particular waterway is no longer of commercial value, it may be of vital importance in other ways. In short, waterways must not be considered purely as navigations, but in relation to the whole of the country's water problem.

Large Scale Plans

Without a full survey it would be impossible to make any hard and fast proposals for the revival and extension of the waterways. Neither can costing be considered here. The schemes and recommendations which follow must, therefore, be taken purely as tentative and hopeful suggestions.

Any proposals for canal reconstruction must be based largely on some national, long-term economic objective. If that objective is mainly to stimulate foreign trade, then the canal system should concentrate on the transport of goods from the great inland industrial centres to the main ports. This can best be effected by developing the Cross. Our present, overcentralized economy, dependent as it is on export markets, would naturally tend to concentrate exclusively on the Cross and a few other main waterways, while ruthlessly abandoning the rest—"cutting out the dead wood," as it is termed. This would be a great mistake because, as we have already seen, canals have other uses than transport. Nor should we—or, indeed, can we—continue to exist on export markets alone. If we attempt to do so our civilization is doomed. Decentralization is long overdue. It means a return to a regional framework of economy based, partly at least, on home food production. Therefore, though the development of the Cross might form part of a broad scheme of canal resuscitation, it is not enough. Mr. L. T. C. Rolt expresses the matter well in his APRR Report:

> " The fact that a waterway does not correspond with the present trade routes is not necessarily a conclusive argument for its abandonment as a navigation. Present trade routes may alter radically within the next few decades; they have evolved to meet the needs of an over-centralized economy based on expanding overseas trade. This period of expansion is over, and the future may witness the re-development of internal resources, the return to a regional economy and a more equable distribution of population. The APRR Broadsheet 5, for example, stresses the need for fresh food, and outlines methods of fulfilling this need by developing agricultural zones round towns as larders for those towns, thus not only narrowing the gap between producer and consumer, but at the same time restoring

* Discussing this subject with a lock-keeper at Hurleston Junction, the author roughly calculated that along a mile length of canal above the junction there were enough cows to consume 4,000 gallons of water on a hot day, allowing 15 gallons per thirsty cow.

the organic relationship between town and country. Many canals, which at present serve little or no useful purpose, might become of great value in such an economy precisely because they were originally built to serve the needs of the similar regional economy which existed before the Industrial Revolution. Their tortuous character was determined, not only by the desire to save locks and earthworks, but also by Brindley's declared axiom that the canal should serve the widest possible rural area. Local records show that village wharves, now disused, once formed centres of local activity. Boats loaded farm and market garden produce for the towns, and returned with coal, lime and—in compliance with the rule of return—stable manure, blood and slaughter house offal, ashes, shoddy, night-soil and other urban wastes. The canals are admirably fitted to play this part again. . . ."

The chief stimulus behind that great movement, which dug thousands of miles of waterway out of the heavy earth by shovel and human muscle alone within a few decades, was the hope of personal gain. We are unlikely, under nationalization, to obtain such a stimulus in the future. Some other stimulus is needed today. It can only be based on the disinterested enthusiasm and energy of government authorities and private representative groups who are able to rouse the rest of the population by sound leadership and the propagating of their vision. If we do not yet possess the enthusiasm and enterprise of the past, we do at least possess, to our advantage, something which the past had not—enormously powerful technical aids.

The Cross

The biggest idea to come from any official body was that expressed in the twelve-volume report presented by the Royal Commission on Waterways which sat between 1906 and 1910. The Commission proposed that the waterways should be developed and enlarged under state control and that, before anything else, the Cross or Four River Scheme should be tackled. The scheme covers the following main routes:

Route A. Birmingham and Leicester to London.
Route B. Leicester, Burton and Nottingham to the Humber.
Route C. Wolverhampton and Birmingham to the Mersey.
Route D. Wolverhampton and Birmingham to the Severn.

The Commission stated that "if these four main routes were put under single control and brought up to date, and if adequate improvements were made in the minor canals that feed them or other means adopted of connecting mines and industrial centres with the main routes, the result would be great benefit to the trade of the country." The Commission came to no definite conclusion about the carrying capacity of the Cross but referred repeatedly to the 100-ton and 300-ton standard boats. (The present narrow boat and its butty between them take about 60 tons.) It was the opinion of Mr. R. B. Dunwoody, who prepared Volume X of the report, that adequate water supplies are available to open up the waterways of the Cross as shown on the map on the next page. (Acknowledgment is due to Mr. J. S. Nettlefold, who prepared the original map on which this one is based, for his work *Garden Cities and Canals*.)

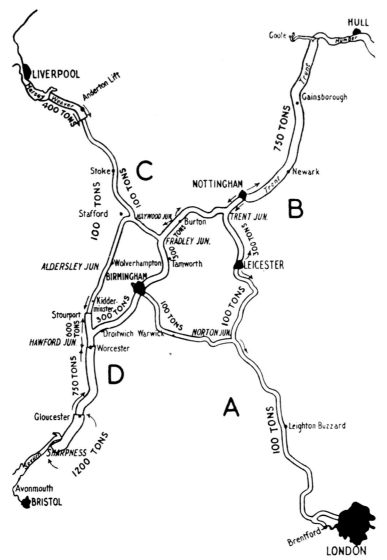

160, the Cross or Four River Scheme, a map from J. S. Nettlefold's "Garden Cities and Canals" based on the proposals of the 1906 Royal Commission's Report for the development of the Cross; the tonnages indicate the proposed standards; all locks, lifts or inclined planes would take trains of barges. (Opposite) 161, J. F. Pownall's Grand Contour Canal.

The Grand Contour Canal

The most visionary scheme to come from an individual is that of Mr. J. F. Pownall, described in his work, *The Projected Grand Contour Canal to Connect with Estuaries and Canals in England*, in which he writes:

" Through the heart of England there runs a *natural canal line*, as I shall term it. This is a line so naturally favourable for canal construction that a canal can follow it easily for many miles at a time whilst remaining throughout on the same level. The old canal surveyors saw this line. They utilized it in many parts of the country to secure long reaches of canal on a single level, but being limited to direct observation of the land, they failed to observe it as other than special to the several localities in which they worked. The natural canal line is an extended feature nevertheless, and it may be made out clearly by the aid of modern contour maps with their great power of revealing land structure. The natural line is determined by a special land structure, arising from uniform erosion.

". . . the contour of 300 feet runs nearly continuously right through the country. . . . A canal by following this contour would therefore proceed right through the country solely on the one level . . . it (also) proceeds in direct

Grand Contour Canal at the level of 310 feet

Existing Canals at other levels

Proposed Canals at other levels

Conduit Extensions at 310 feet (for water distribution)

Vessel lifts down to sea level, or to low level stated L^{SL} or L^{100}

Towns served at the 310 feet level in italics

reaches for long distances at a time. . . . The natural canal line creates the remarkable possibility, never before known, of having a canal to go through the length of the country and serve the great industrial areas without any variation from the one level.

"As compared with a canal at varying levels, the ultimate carrying capacity of a one-level canal would be enormous, and the cost of working traffic along it would be far less because of the avoidance of the loss of time and water in locking, and especially by reason of the freedom for towing in trains. Vessels which ply only on the one level can be of various special types not elsewhere possible. Vessels can be devised to convey economically large built-up fabrications and cargo which bulks large for its weight and to supply important new categories of transport service. Moreover, a slow artificial current could be created without difficulty and without impeding navigation, and thus a one-level canal could be used as a water distributor. There being no locks, it could be used freely by recreational craft.

"These are very great advantages. The writer has therefore worked out a project for a new canal system, the Grand Contour Canal, to be uniformly level at 310 ft. above sea level, and to serve London, Bristol, Southampton, Birmingham, Manchester, Leeds and Newcastle. All the existing canals would be effective branches from it. The waterway would be large enough to accommodate coastal vessels of a fair size, and the Grand Contour Canal would form with all estuaries and coastal routes one system for coastal vessels. The Grand Contour Canal would become the primary water distributor of the country.

"It would serve directly, or by waterway connections, nearly all the great industrial areas of the country. Birmingham, Bradford, and many other towns would be served at the level of 310 ft., and by using the many existing canal reaches at a single level, a large number of towns would be served with only one change in level, by vessel lift, from 310 ft.

"It is proposed provisionally that the waterway should be 30 metres or 100 ft. wide at the top, that the depth should be about 17 ft. and the clear headway 25 ft.

"Water-buses will find a place on the 310 ft. level, and pleasure vessels in various types will conduct excursions up to the degree of long tours through the country.

"Along the Grand Contour Canal there will be formed a special layer in the bed, possibly of gravel, and above any clay puddle that may be placed. In this layer pipelines for the transport of commercial liquids and gases would be embedded. . . . The fluids which would be piped would include petroleum products, salts in solution, trade wastes, coal gas, compressed air and oxygen.

"Holiday-makers who navigate the Grand Contour Canal in yachts or launches will observe how well the canal fits into the countryside. The heavy works are mostly in the form of tunnel. Large aqueducts are few and will usually be high bank with turfed or timbered slopes. Precisely because it expresses a natural feature, the Contour Canal will lie unobtrusively on the land and will have a characteristic scenery of its own. It will most often be seen as a quiet ribbon of water winding along at the foot of an escarpment of sorts on one side, whilst the land falls away gently on the other side."

This is a remarkable and imaginative proposal and one which should certainly be considered by the authorities. No doubt Treasury-bound officialdom will deride such splendid ideas and pose the eternal question: " Where is the money to come from ?" Any reformer's answer must always be a definition of the word Cost—" The total real cost of any project is not finally a question of money, since money should be merely a measuring system, but the amount of real wealth consumed by those concerned with that project during its execution. If that real wealth can be made available, the project can be accomplished. What is physically possible *must be* financially possible."

General Recommendations

The following general recommendations for canal revival are a composite based on various sources, including the Rolt Report and the Memorandum of the Inland Waterways Association presented in 1947 to the Minister of Transport. It is supported by the writer's own reflections which are based on personal observation over a number of months on some fifteen different navigations.

Dredging.—About 75 per cent. of all canals are in urgent need of dredging. This should at once be carried out to a universal minimum depth of 5 ft. With modern equipment a complete programme of dredging is not a large operation and would soon show returns in the increased loads which could be carried and the higher speeds of delivery. (On many canals 34-ton boats can now only carry 25 tons and great delay is caused by boats getting " stemmed up "—*i.e.*, going hard aground.)

Strengthening of Banks.—The only effective way of preventing silting in future is by (1) reinforcement of the banks, preferably with *in situ* or pre-cast concrete at all points where erosion takes place; (2) the planting of the common rush on the margins of waterways of shelving section; (3) the building in future of hull forms and channels of correct depth and cross-section arrived at by study and experiment.

Water Supply.—Where water supplies are inadequate, reservoirs should be cleaned and enlarged and waste should be prevented by adequate puddling and lock maintenance and the increased provision of side-pounds at locks.

Locks.—Locks and their gates were never set out in the past with precision and their dimensions vary by inches. The result is that new lock-gates have to be specially made in each case. Locks and their gates should be standardized to the greatest possible extent in order that new parts may be supplied from a prefabricated stock. Where actual or potential traffic justifies enlargement, the number of locks should be reduced and depth increased. Where suitable, lifts should be installed in place of existing flights of locks.

Plant and Wharfage.—This should also be standardized as far as possible. Most existing plant and equipment is obsolete, inefficient and inadequate. New cranage and handling plant is especially needed; far too much manual labour is now used in handling canal traffic. The Weaver Navigation is one of the few which has installed modern plant, and has thereby halved its handling costs. Wharfage is also inadequate, out-of-date, and its general unsightliness does not entice business. Especially needed are new coal wharves, for even present tonnage of coal shipped by canal bears no relation to loading facilities.

Two-way Loading.—One of the main reasons why canal carriers work with so narrow a margin of profit is that boats travel empty in one direction far too often. By proper organization this can be avoided. An essential part of reorganization should be the establishment of base warehouses or dumps at all points between which there is a regular flow of traffic so that craft can pick up a load at any time if there is no current load available. Distribution heads should also be set up, consisting of transit sheds, a garage for lorries and a rail connection if possible.

Canal Craft.—Though the maximum size will depend on the programme of canal enlargement, the larger the boat, within limits, the better. Nevertheless it is wrong to dismiss the whole of the narrow boat system as obsolete and to argue that the only alternative to immediate large-scale reconstruction is abandonment. The present narrow boat has some advantages, for on certain hauls larger craft would involve the pooling of cargoes between canal users, resulting in delays in transit, whereas the smaller boat can carry a consignment of convenient size to be handled by one trader and so proceed directly to the trader's wharf. Generalization on this question is unwise. In handling waterborne cargoes the use of the road-rail container principle should be considered. In the case of the standard narrow boat, containers would be of welded steel loading seven to a pair of boats.

Control of Pollution.—On many canals pollution by trade wastes and effluents is so bad that no aquatic life of any kind can survive in them. Rigorous control should be exercised over both domestic and industrial pollution, and purification plant should be installed where necessary.

Weed Control.—Research into weed growth is urgently needed so that this can be controlled. More traffic on the canals is, however, the best weed killer.

Administration.—The present organization of the Docks and Inland Waterways Executive in four areas is quite arbitrary. The most natural form of organization would be regional, defined by the main catchment areas. In each region a Catchment Board should be responsible for all problems relating to the use, disposal and conservation of water resources within their area. On the Boards should be representatives of commercial water transport, pleasure transport, local fisheries, local agriculture, water supply and drainage, local and regional town and country planning. If the present system of tolls is maintained a national scale should be instituted and all redundant gauging points eliminated. The alternative should be considered of instituting a tax system, as organized on the roads.

Carrying Trade.—The carrying industry has always been disorganized and latterly the state of the canals has not encouraged its improvement and expansion. Before nationalization there were about six hundred separate and independent carriers with fleets ranging from one to three hundred craft, most of them specializing in one type of cargo. Since nationalization many of the larger carrying companies, such as the Grand Union, and Fellows, Morton and Clayton, have been, or are, in the process of being nationalized. Complete nationalization of carriage is probably a bad thing and would have a morally depressing effect, just as it would be a bad thing to nationalize all the boat-building yards which have been built up by working men of character and initiative with great pride in their craft. Independent carriers and boat-builders should be helped and encouraged by the Government.

Boatmen's Amenities and Conditions.—The boatman's life is a healthy but a hard one, and is at present unmitigated by any amenity, except the ancient canal inn. Washing, sanitary, laundry, health, shopping, canteen and general welfare facilities should be established at key points along the main routes, designed on a par with the Miners' Welfare buildings. Drastic measures such as these are urgently needed to prevent withdrawal from the canals. At present boatmen are paid solely on tonnage and distance, and work is irregular. A regular weekly wage with the addition of tonnage bonus should be paid. A system of schooling for the long-distance boatmen's children should be organized without removing the children from their boat homes and so disrupting family life. Better school facilities should be established at canal terminals. The traditional rose and castle decorations and other boating traditions should be encouraged. This is no sentimental belief. By such traditions better types are attracted to the Cut and pride in the boats is stimulated with resulting careful maintenance and lower upkeep costs. At present nationalized boats are being painted a uniform blue and yellow, an unimaginative and short-sighted policy and one which is universally unpopular, especially among the boaters themselves. As the boatwomen declare, " We have never had gardens, but we had our roses," or referring to the new style, " The boats are our homes. Who wants to live in them Yeller Perils ?"

Towpaths.—These should be declared public rights of way, whether they are still used for navigational purposes or not, and should be considered as part of a national footpath system—always provided, of course, that the mischievous and predatory tendencies of the public can be controlled.

Canal Monuments.—The canals contain many structures of historic and æsthetic value, especially bridges, of which there are literally hundreds of fine design. A special Government survey should be made of these with the object of preserving them under the Town and Country Planning Act of 1947. At the moment they are little known and there is grave danger that many of them will be thoughtlessly demolished by local authorities. This vandalism is happening at the present time to many of Telford's superb little bridges on the Welsh Section of the Shropshire Union and a similar threat overhangs the bridges of the Rochdale Canal.

Survey.—Apart from immediate dredging, no long-term plans can be laid for the use of the canals without a full survey. This should be organized at once to provide the following information:

(1) Commercial and pleasure traffic at present carried.

(2) Potential commercial and pleasure traffic.

(3) Whether the waterway is in good navigable condition, and if not what steps would be necessary to make it so.

(4) Whether the water supply is adequate to handle (a) existing, (b) potential traffic, and, if not, what steps would be necessary to ensure adequate supply.

(5) Whether potential traffic justifies constructional enlargement or improvement additional to the restoration to good order of existing facilities.

(6) Whether wharfage and handling facilities are adequate, and, if not, how they might be improved.

(7) How, if the waterway were to be abandoned, the amenities, drainage, and water-supply problems of the area would be affected.

(8) The extent to which waterways can be associated with military defence, modern trading estates, new power stations, and all new town planning schemes as part of a general policy of decentralization.

Publicity.—A proper public relations and publicity department both for trade and pleasure should be instituted to popularize and make known the existence, value and advantages of the waterways both for trade and pleasure, on a par with those of railways and airlines.

Canals for Pleasure.—Precisely those waterways which, because they pass through predominantly rural areas, are unlikely to carry a heavy commercial traffic, would prove of the greatest value in meeting the growing demand for holiday amenities. Many of those waterways are not only of the greatest scenic beauty but contain historical, architectural and engineering structures of a monumental quality. They are also admirably placed in relation to areas of dense population. Canals which are obviously most suitable for immediate development as tourist attractions are: the Lancaster, the Shropshire Union, the Kennet and Avon, the Stratford, the Basingstoke, the Macclesfield and Peak Forest, the Grantham, the Ashby. None of these would require great capital expenditure in order to be restored. Organized canal cruising could be developed and publicized to encourage foreign visitors (See Britain by Canal). Many countries, notably France and Holland, derive large incomes from this source. Small boat basins should be provided in suitable places near large towns where private boats can be safely moored. Canals where they pass through towns should be considered in relation to local planning and the best use made of their scenic assets by the planting of gardens and erection of restaurants and recreational centres along their banks. A particular case in this respect is the Paddington Basin in London, at present a forlorn spot but one with inherent possibilities as London's Venice, to give it Browning's title. The canals of Gothenburg provide excellent examples for emulation.

Conclusion

" There is a great opportunity before the Government completely to revolutionize at surprisingly small expenditure the management of a national asset extending all over the land and capable of bettering the life of the people at many different points: a national asset which has been, to an extent hardly to be paralleled elsewhere, brought near to a point of destruction by public ignorance and inertia and the manipulations of hostile parties. Upon our inland waterways converge, as in few other places, the arguments of low cost and human amenity. No Government representing on a broad basis the people of England can possibly allow them to go to waste; can possibly do other than restore and free them: for an efficient system could, directly or indirectly, lower the real cost of almost every commodity, and bring much happiness to the larger part than half of our population which lives near some section of it." (Memorandum of the Inland Waterways Association presented to the Minister of Transport, 1947.)

162

On the opposite page and elsewhere in this book the possible uses of canals for pleasure have been discussed. These final pages illustrate some of the points made, and indicate how pleasurable the canals could be. They also show how the canals have been used for pleasure purposes in the past, how they are now so used to a very limited extent, and how they could be so used in the future. The pictures show that our neglected canals, originally intended for commercial traffic and now grown weedy and silted in the country and mere stinking ditches in the towns, could, with relatively little expense, be revitalised to become delightful national linear parks—the kind of amenity we now so badly need. 162 (above), the Welsh Section of the Shropshire Union Canal in the lovely Vale of Llangollen. This canal is now used almost entirely as a feeder for the main line and provides an example of a canal which should be fully developed for pleasure since it cannot, in any case, be closed down. On the few miles between Llangollen and the intake from the River Dee at the Horse Shoe Falls, the canal is indeed now being used for this purpose, for here in the summer months run Mr. Robert's horse-drawn pleasure boats. His is the kind of private enterprise which deserves encouragement.

163

164

Views which show how pleasurable canal travel could be for those who delight in landscapes where man-made adjuncts enhance the natural scene. 163, a sloping stone bridge in the Vale of Llangollen. 164, the stone bridge in Teddesley Park on the Staffordshire and Worcestershire Canal—an elaborate Gentleman's Estate type of bridge in contrast to the usual, purely functional but no less attractive type. 165, towpath, little stone bridge and rocky cutting above Llangollen. 166, the Grand Union in Cassiobury Park, Watford. 167, on the Welsh section of the Shropshire Union just above Hurleston Junction. 168, the semi-derelict Basingstoke Canal, still privately owned.

166

169

170

171

169, *pleasure canal boats sketched at Paddington Basin in 1849.*
pleasure boats meet at the Welsh border on the Shropshire Un
larger boat is a converted army bridge pontoon in which the author
the canals; its shallow draft was a great advantage. 171, *a schoo*
in a hired Narrow Boat passing a rare rowing boat station establ
Tettenhall on the Staffordshire and Worcestershire Canal since
century. 172, *a Narrow Boat converted into a permanent home ly*
turf-sided lock, a rare and early type, on the Kennet and Avon Na

173

174

173, Lord Burlington's garden at Chiswick, an example of a canal built entirely for decorative and pleasure purposes.
174, a sketch by Gordon Cullen suggesting the way a canal in the country might be treated today. To lay out the
canals as linear parks is a job for the landscape architect. There are many things he will have to avoid—the planning
of car parks along the canal-side; too much regimentation of nature by fencing her off or by laying down asphalt paths
in straight lines; the designing of tea gardens in a formal, unimaginative, municipal park style; the littering of the tow
path with litter baskets and prim, puritanical benches; the thoughtless cutting of trees and so on. There are many
things he will have to aim at—to use the water itself as much as possible for canal structures such as cafés; to design
buildings like boathouses with lightness, gaiety and charm, to form part of the picture as a whole; to use the water itself,
with its moving reflections, as decoration; to blend buildings and canal furniture with the natural character of the site.

117

175

*English canals are at their worst in towns. Buildings turn their rears disdainfully, discharging stinking effluents. Local knowledge
is needed to pilot craft safely between sunken reefs of tin cans, brickbats and skeletal remains. No one seems to be responsible.
Here is British squalor at its most horrific. We must now use canals in towns to form delightful strip parks, because water
provides the landscape architect with his most useful material. 175, the Paddington Basin is to-day a sorry and unkempt sight,
but it has great inherent possibilities for development as London's Little Venice; a few more trees, some grass and flowers, a clearance
of rubbish, a bright café or two, a little bunting and plenty of fresh paint would make all the difference. 176, shows, by odious
comparison, a colourful picture of a barge café on a canal in Gothenburg, Sweden, where the old canals are linked with the park system of
the town. 177, a suggestion by Gordon Cullen on how to treat an urban canal where the local pub steps down to a waterside terrace.*

Short Chronology of Canals

1121 *The Fossdyke Canal, Lincolnshire, an old Roman work, scoured out by Henry I.*

1481 *Locks known to the Italians.*

1566 *Exeter Canal opened.*

1716 *James Brindley born.*

1736 *Francis, Duke of Bridgewater, born.*

1745 *William Jessop born.*

1755 *Act for St. Helens, or Sankey, Canal.*

1757 *Thomas Telford born.*

1761 *Bridgewater Canal from Worsley to Manchester completed.*
John Rennie born.

1766 *First sod of Grand Trunk (Trent and Mersey) Canal cut by Josiah Wedgwood, July 26.*

1767 *Bridgewater Canal from Longford Bridge to Runcorn opened.*

1768 *Acts for Coventry, Droitwich and Birmingham Canal Navigations.*

1769 *Act for Oxford Canal.*

1770 *Act for Leeds and Liverpool Canal.*

1771 *Acts for Chesterfield and Bradford Canal.*

1772 *Staffordshire and Worcestershire Canal completed.*
Brindley died.

1777 *Harecastle Old Tunnel opened.*

1778 *Act for Basingstoke Canal.*

1780 *Act for Thames and Severn Canal.*

1782 *Fossdyke Canal deepened to 3 ft. 6 in.*

1788 *Act for Shropshire Canal.*
First inclined plane in England made by William Reynolds on Ketley Canal in Shropshire, a copper medal being struck to commemorate it.
Sapperton Tunnel on summit level of Thames and Severn Canal visited by George III when in course of construction.

1789 *Acts for Andover and Cromford Canals.*
First attempt at using steam power on canals made on Forth and Clyde Canal with Symington's boat.

1790 *Oxford Canal finally completed and opened to Oxford on January 1 amidst public rejoicing.*
Grand Junction Canal begun.

1791 *At least eight canal Acts passed this year.*

1792 *At least eight more Acts passed.*

1793 *At least twenty-one Acts passed, including that for the Grand Junction.*

1794 *At least twenty-four Acts passed, including those for the Kennet and Avon and the Rochdale.*

1795 *Six Acts passed.*

1796 *Four Acts passed.*

1799 *Kennet and Avon Canal opened.*

1801 *Chirk Aqueduct completed.*

1803 *Duke of Bridgewater died.*
Pontcysyllte Aqueduct completed.
The Northampton Mercury of December 24, describing the Smithfield Cattle Show, says, " Some of the oxen were uncommonly fine in their proportions. The oxen of Mr. Westcar (of Aylesbury) were universally allowed to be great beauties. They have also the advantage over those which travelled to town, that they were brought up unfatigued by their journey, as Mr. Westcar lives near the Grand Junction Canal."

1806 *The Times of December 19 contains the following announcement: " The first division of the troops that are to proceed by Paddington Canal to Liverpool, and thence by transports for Dublin, will leave Paddington today, and will be followed by others tomorrow and on Sunday. By this mode of conveyance the men will be only seven days in reaching Liverpool."*

1809 *Patent perpendicular lift for canal boats, invented by John Woodhouse, erected on the Worcester and Birmingham Canal at Tardebigge.*

1812 *Act for Regent's Canal.*

1820 *Regent's Canal opened.*

1826 *Acts for Birmingham and Liverpool Junction Canal and Macclesfield Canal.*

1827 *Gloucester and Berkeley Ship Canal completed.*

1829 *Oxford Canal improvements by Telford commenced for shortening distance between Napton and Braunston by 14 miles.*

1834 *Thomas Telford died.*

1836 *Steam tugs used on Aire and Calder Navigation.*

1840 *Act to provide for keeping the peace on canals and navigable rivers.*

1845 *Five canals bought by railway companies, including Thames and Medway Canal, part of canal being converted into a railway.*
Act passed to enable canal companies to become carriers.
Leeds and Liverpool Canal Co. become carriers.

1846-1848 *Some twenty-three canals purchased by, leased to, or amalgamated with railway companies.*

1863 *Worcester and Birmingham Canal passes into the hands of a receiver.*

1864 *Last dividend paid by Thames and Severn Canal.*

1868 *Fenny Compton Tunnel (1,200 yds. long), on summit level of Oxford Canal, removed and replaced by a cutting.*
Act for abandonment of Wey and Arun Junction Canal.

1875 *Anderton hydraulic lift from River Weaver to Trent and Mersey Canal completed.*

1877 *Act passed for the registration and regulation of canal boats used as dwellings. Amended 1884.*

1879 *Act for Slough Branch of Grand Junction Canal.*

1894 *Manchester Ship Canal opened for traffic, January 1.*

1917 *Canals come under national war-time control.*

1929 *Merging of Grand Junction, Regent's Canal, Warwick and Napton and Warwick and Birmingham Canals as the Grand Union.*

1932 *Grand Union Canal Co. spend £1,000,000, as part of scheme to combat depression, on general improvements, including reinforcement of banks with concrete piling and new locks near Warwick, but fail to secure enough money to complete a dredging programme.*

1936 *Newtown Arm of Shropshire Union burst.*

1944 *Huddersfield Narrow Canal and Newtown Arm abandoned.*

1948 *All canals under national control during war, as well as all railway-owned canals nationalized under new Transport Act.*

Bibliography

Historical Account of the Navigable Rivers, Canals and Railways of Great Britain as a Reference to Nichols, Priestley and Walker's New Map of Inland Navigation. By Joseph Priestley. (Longman, Rees, Orme, Brown and Green, 1831). An important standard work of historical reference, but not for light reading. Contains small map, and navigation sections.

Lives of the Engineers. By Dr. Samuel Smiles. Famous standard work to be read preferably in the original three volume edition, published by John Murray in 1861, on account of the many engravings it contains. Includes the lives of such canal men as Brindley, Telford and Rennie.

Bradshaw's Canals and Navigable Rivers of England and Wales. Edited by H. R. de Salis. (Henry Blacklock, last edition 1928.) Famous standard work. Very useful guide giving descriptions of the various canals and navigations, distances, lock tables, tunnel lengths and so on. Contains map. Rare.

Inland Waterways of Great Britain and Northern Ireland. By Lewis A. Edwards. (Imray, 1950). Far less comprehensive than Bradshaw, but useful to canal and river voyagers. Map.

Chronology of Inland Navigation. By H. R. de Salis. (E. and F. N. Spon, 1897.) Rare book of interest to the canal historian.

Our Waterways. By V. A. Forbes and W. H. R. Ashford. (John Murray, 1906.) Past, present and future of British rivers and canals, especially in relation to water conservancy. An important and interesting work. Map.

Report of the Royal Commission on Canals. (H.M.S.O., 1906-1910.) Twelve volumes of evidence and proposals, much of it of great interest. Rare.

Garden Cities and Canals. By J. S. Nettlefold. (St. Catherine Press, 1914). Plea for canal development in relation to garden cities. Of value in giving précis of 1906 Royal Commission Report.

The Projected Grand Contour Canal. By J. F. Pownall. (Cotterel, 1942.) An individual's imaginative proposal for a large new canal traversing England at one level.

Memorandum Presented to the Minister of Transport. (Inland Waterways Association, 11, Gower St., W.1. 1947.) The case for canal revival presented.

Inland Waterways. Prepared by L. T. C. Rolt. (Association for Planning and Regional Reconstruction, Report R41, 1946.) History, survey, principles of waterway construction, water supply and maintenance, future of abandoned canals, recommendations. An important document.

The Flower of Gloster. By E. Temple Thurston. (Williams and Norgate, 1911). Light travelogue of a canal journey in a Narrow Boat.

Narrow Boat. By L. T. C. Rolt (Eyre and Spottiswoode, 1944.) Best selling canal travelogue of a more serious and informative nature than Thurston's. Largely responsible for the current interest in canals and their revival.

The Development of Transportation in Modern England. By W. T. Jackman. (Cambridge University Press, 1914, two volumes.) Deals with road, rail and waterway transport up to the early railway age and includes several excellent chapters on canals.

Our Canal Population: A Cry from the Boat Cabins. By George Smith. (Haughton, 1875.) A vivid social document, largely a collection of newspaper articles pleading for improvement of conditions of canal boaters. Smith was responsible for the passing of the 1877 and 1884 Canal Boats Acts.

The Rose and Castle. By Barbara Jones. (Article in the *Architectural Review*, December, 1946.) Excellent article on traditional Narrow Boat decoration with drawings in colour.

Inland Waterways of England. By L. T. C. Rolt. (Allen and Unwin.) Summary of waterway history, notable engineering works, waterway maintenance, types of boats, life of the boaters. A useful contribution to social history. Illustrated. *In preparation.*

The Story of British Canals. By C. E. R. Hadfield. (Phœnix House.) Comprehensive and erudite history up to the present day, based on original records. Illustrated. Numerous maps.

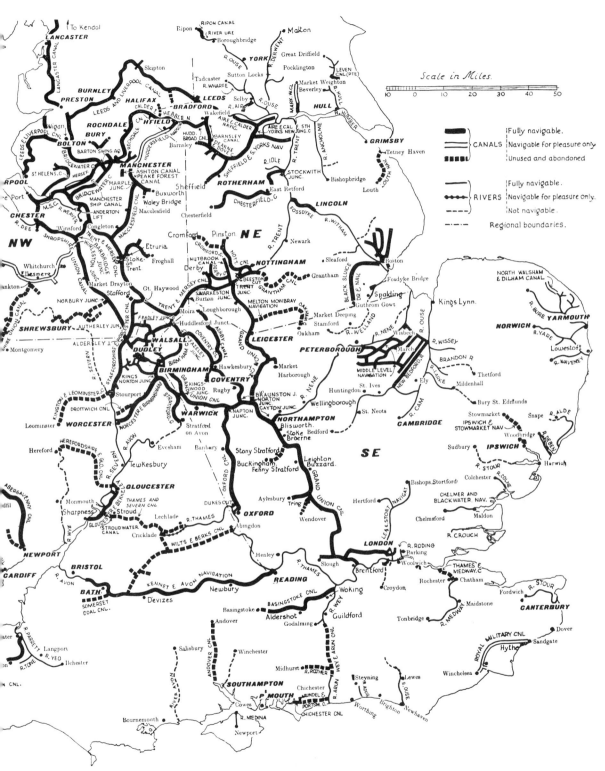

178, map of the English Canal System.

Index

All references are to pages of the book. The numbers of illustrations are set in italics within brackets after their page numbers.

179, Paddington Basin on the Regent's Canal, from an engraving of 1828.